I0802020

CENTRAL MINNESOTA BEER

CENTRAL MINNESOTA BEER

A History

JACOB LAXEN

AMERICAN PALATE

Published by American Palate
A Division of The History Press
Charleston, SC
www.historypress.com

Front cover: An evening look at University Bridge in St. Cloud, Minnesota. The bridge, which is located over the Mississippi River, connects St. Cloud and passes the edge of St. Cloud State University. *Photograph by Central Minnesota freelance photographer Kimm Anderson.*

First published 2020

Manufactured in the United States

ISBN 9781467142236

Library of Congress Control Number: 2020930363

Notice: The information in this book is true and complete to the best of our knowledge. It is offered without guarantee on the part of the author or The History Press. The author and The History Press disclaim all liability in connection with the use of this book.

CONTENTS

PREFACE

As a *St. Cloud Times* reporter, I covered the reemergence of beer in Central Minnesota. I celebrated many of the breweries' grand openings and new beer releases. I was present when liquor stores massively expanded their beer selections and bars doubled their number of tap handles. Options expanded for beer geeks, and it caused me to study the history of brewing in the same communities that I had previously covered.

To many like myself, Central Minnesota is a region where Minnesotans receive college educations. My alma mater, St. Cloud State University, is the state's second-largest college behind the University of Minnesota. The nearby town of St. Joseph attracts thousands to St. John's University and the College of St. Benedicts. St. Cloud Technical and Community College also has a large annual enrollment. For many other Minnesotans, Central Minnesota is a cabin and camping destination, with a number of the large lakes—this is true in my case as well. I grew up in the Twin Cities' suburb of Shakopee, which houses the country's largest beer malt distributor, but I spent nearly every summer weekend of my childhood in our RV at El Rancho Manana Campground near Cold Spring. I remember passing near the Cold Spring Brewery on the way, having no idea just how much history it had. Other members of my family have long lived in the Central Minnesota area.

I worked for two stints at the *St. Cloud Times*. First, I was a sports reporter for several years while I was attending St. Cloud State University; I was hired by the newspaper's longest-tenured sports editor, Dave DeLand. This experience gave me a deeper understanding of St. Cloud as well as the cultures and traditions of the surrounding communities. I was not drinking very good beer at this time. My second stint, however, came during the country's craft beer revolution of the 2010s. I began exploring different beers with my drinking buddies and contributors to this book—professor and photographer Andrew Webster and archivist Adam "Shmitty" Smith. I covered a number of topics during this stint, including Central Minnesota's food and beverage scene. I was even briefly advertised on a billboard off Division Street. I learned a lot from the columns of Bruce LeBlanc, a local homebrew pioneer who wrote a guest chapter for this book.

My beer coverage in St. Cloud extended beyond Central Minnesota. *St. Cloud Times*'s parent company, *USA Today*, published my profiles on Sam Adams founder Jim Koch; the American IPA pioneers at Russian River Brewing; the Fat Tire and sour pioneers from New Belgium; and the founders of the storied Alaskan Brewing. They also published my behind-the-scenes look at how Ballast Point became the first craft brewery that was sold for $1 billion and my articles about Budweiser's nationwide shopping spree of craft breweries and controversial Super Bowl commercials dissing craft beer and "pumpkin peach ales." I even got to interview former professional wrestler "Stone Cold" Steve Austin and NBA star Chris Bosh about their passions for beer in the old *St. Cloud Times* office. Craft beer samples made across the country began showing up in my mailboxes at my office and home. I even received a bottle of the super rare Sam Adams Utopia—which I proceeded to drop and shatter, only getting a few sips off of the bottle's glass shards.

I eventually transferred to the beer hub of Fort Collins, Colorado, where I continue to cover the beer scene closely. The area oddly had a large impact on Central Minnesota's beer revival. Fort Collins houses a major Budweiser brewery, New Belgium Brewing, Odell Brewing, Funkwerks and a number of other breweries—it is a beer heaven. But I have never forgotten Central Minnesota and its beer history. Beer has been an integral part of politics, business and culture in the region for more than a century. The goal of this book is to tell the tale of Central Minnesota brewing and how it continues to flourish with bountiful water sources today.

INTRODUCTION

In the center of the Land of Ten Thousand Lakes rests a bounty of water. The Mississippi River cuts through the heart of Central Minnesota, picking up steam from its humble beginnings in the shallow Lake Itasca, where it starts its 2,348-mile journey downstream to the Gulf of Mexico. Central Minnesota also has sparkling springs that are fed by glacial lakes, flowing tributary rivers and giant lakes the size of Paul Bunyan's footprint.

For generations, various Native American tribes collected resources in and around Central Minnesota's waterways. Later, explorers journaled their amazement and wonder at the area's various waterways; European settlers followed in the mid-1800s. The bountiful waterways were the perfect sources for brewing beer. A large influx of German settlers brought the German culture of brewing to the area. Swiss and Hungarian immigrants also had a significant impact on early Central Minnesota brewing. The settlers were accustomed to Europe's industrial culture, where drinking beer was safer than drinking the bacteria-filled water that was available at the time—the heating process of brewing kills off bacteria and parasites in water. By the turn of the twentieth century, beer was advertised in Central Minnesota newspapers as a medicine to aid digestion and as a healthy substitute for coffee. Historians say people of all ages drank prior to Prohibition.

Fires burned down many of Central Minnesota's earliest breweries. Some empires were ruined by Prohibition, and others fizzled out shortly after the nationwide ban on alcohol, when significantly stricter laws and regulations were placed on the industry. But through thick and thin, one Central

Minnesota brewery endured. Today, the Cold Spring Brewing Company operates in the same spot as it did when Michael Sargl first brewed there with a kettle in 1874—now under the Third Street Brewhouse label.

Brewpubs brought a new beer culture to Central Minnesota in the mid-1990s, and one St. Cloud brewery spread the Granite City's culture and its beers across the country. A new beer culture took hold in Minnesota, thanks to a piece of 2011 state legislation known as the "Surly Bill," named after the popular Twin Cities brewery that legally challenged the existing laws. The restrictive laws that had once forced the number of Minnesota breweries to dwindle down to just four were overturned, and Minnesota's breweries were revived to number more than one hundred. The North Star State has been nationally revered for its growing beer community, regularly claiming medals at the annual Great American Beer Festival. Central Minnesota is once again using its bountiful waterways to make beer. Breweries have popped up across the region, giving towns—both large and small—taprooms that operate with a much more relaxed vibe than a traditional bar.

Beaver Island's Sweet Mississippi, Third Street Brewhouse's Minnesota Gold, Granite City's Bennie Bock and Bad Habit Brewing's Dark Addiction are among the beers that have joined other Central Minnesota legacy brands like St. Cloud Brewing Company's Old Heidelberger, Pitzl Brewing's Weiner Lager, Cold Spring Pep, Billy Beer, Elvira's Night Brew and Gluek. An annual winter beer festival at the St. Cloud Convention Center now draws thousands annually. At this festival, the rare collaborative nature of the brewing community is put on display. Rival breweries and distributors come together for one big party, which is far from limited to the convention center. St. Cloud bars and restaurants get into the spirit of the beer festival by hosting tap takeovers and tapping rare kegs. A similar outdoor summer festival has also been launched with a focus on hard ciders.

Experimentation drives today's new brewers. Beers made with potatoes, maple syrup and the Scandinavian specialty lefse have been produced in Central Minnesota. Barrel-aging, brut and sour yeasts and unfiltered hazy beers have taken beer geeks in this region by storm—just as they have across the country. And more experimental batches sit in fermentation tanks today. The new craft beer revolution has been fueled by homebrewers who graduated from their garage set-ups to commercial breweries—some of today's most popular beers are just scaled-up versions of past homebrew recipes.

Beer bus tours now have enough stops to take travelers all over Central Minnesota. Some restaurants in the area now host multi-course beer dinners, with each flight strategically paired to accompany each bite. The region's storied homebrew club has seen the induction of a new generation of brewers, and female-specific beer clubs have been launched. Central Minnesota beers have found their way throughout the state and even into neighboring Wisconsin. Beers made in the region can be found throughout the Twin Cities, as well as north in Duluth.

I

CENTRAL MINNESOTA'S EARLIEST BREWERIES

As soon as German settlers made their way to Central Minnesota, they brought their traditional beer recipes with them. Breweries popped up in cities throughout the area, and the earliest breweries were located conveniently next to key water sources, the same lakes and rivers that many Minnesotans enjoy recreationally today.

Commercial brewing started in Minnesota in 1848—a decade before Minnesota became a state—with the Anthony Yoerg Brewing Company in St. Paul. It was located along the Mississippi River, where the Science Museum of Minnesota's parking lot sits today. Yoerg was born in a Bavarian village in Germany, and he immigrated to the United States at the age of nineteen. He first settled in Pittsburgh before later relocating to Galena, Illinois, and St. Paul. Yoerg ran a butcher shop in a German neighborhood in St. Paul, but he later decided to change careers and open a brewery. He was known for aging his beers in caves. The Yoerg brewery continuously operated in the Yoerg family until 1952. The Yoerg brand was reincarnated at a St. Paul brewery in 2018.

Just over a decade after Yoerg launched Minnesota brewing, a commercial brewery was launched just to the north, in Central Minnesota—many would follow. Few would enjoy the longevity of Yoerg Brewing, but they were all important parts of Minnesota's early settlements.

Kraemer Brewing

The honor of being Central Minnesota's first brewer belongs to German immigrant Peter Kraemer. Historical tax records indicate he made five hundred barrels of beer in St. Cloud in 1859, and each barrel contained thirty-one gallons of beer. The Kraemer Brewery was located off a ravine that fed into the south shore of Lake George. Records state that this area was considered to be on the outskirts of St. Cloud at the time. Today, the thought of that is humorous, as the renovated Lake George is the center of the community's events, including a free, weekly summer concert and food truck festival series that draws thousands.

Lake George was much larger back when Kraemer was making beer from its waters. The lake was systematically drained before it was turned into the community hub that it is today. St. Cloud was originally settled for its water supply. According to city records, three separate upper, middle and lower towns were established around two ravines that fed into the Mississippi River. In 1856, the three separate towns united under the name St. Cloud; the town was named after a Paris suburb, which was named in honor of a sixth-century French monk.

Kraemer made a lager beer that required a lengthy fermentation. He wasn't alone in running his beer business. His partner was a fellow German immigrant named Peter Seberger—his last name may sound familiar to St. Cloud residents. Peter Jr., Seberger's son, served as the first mayor of the reorganized St. Cloud and currently has a town park named after him. The Seberger family immigrated to Chicago from Germany before they eventually resettled in Central Minnesota on a Richmond farm.

By 1863, the Kraemer Brewery had increased its yearly production to about 2,600 barrels, which was an average of 50 barrels a week. The original brewery in Central Minnesota didn't last long, as it burned down on the morning of November 24, 1864. The fire caused an estimated $8,000 worth of damage to the five-year-old brewery. Fires were common in early Minnesota breweries. Doug Hoverson, the author of *Land of Amber Waters: The History of Brewing in Minnesota*, told the *St. Cloud Times* that fires were common in this era because of "a perfect storm of combinations." In this era, many breweries were constructed from wood, used wood equipment and used fire for lantern light and heat. During this era, many prohibitionists were also accused of starting the flames in protest.

Kraemer and Seberger decided to never rebuild the Kraemer Brewery. Kraemer went on to become a hotel proprietor, and Seberger pursued other business ventures, but beer has been made in Central Minnesota from the moment they first tapped their lager made with water from Lake George. Little did they know, their original watering hole would someday become the epicenter of the city of St. Cloud.

St. Cloud's Second Brewery

Just before the Kraemer Brewery burned down, another St. Cloud brewery joined the town's beer scene. Frank Funk became a commercial brewer in 1864, making seven barrels of beer at 519 Eighth Avenue North, which today is a residence located a couple blocks away from both St. Cloud Cathedral High School and the Mississippi River. Funk ran the brewery until 1876, when new ownership took over. The operation, now named Remely and Thierry Brewing, increased its production to about one thousand barrels a year. Then, a fire broke out in 1878, causing an estimated $8,000 worth of damage to the brewery. Fortunately, some hops, beer and a vault were reclaimed after the fire.

A new duo took over the Eighth Avenue brewery in 1881. Frank Balder and Nick Weber added a new sixty-five-foot-tall tower to the malt house in 1884 and ramped up production. Weber moved to Montana in 1886, and the brewery became known as the Balder Brewery. Its operation would peak in 1887, when thirteen Balder Brewery employees produced six thousand barrels in just one year. Tax records indicate that Fred Zertler bought the operation from Balder eight years later, in 1895. The brewery closed in 1897 and became a part of St. Cloud's brewing lore.

A Swiss St. Cloud Brewery

Not all of Central Minnesota's early breweries were run by German immigrants. Swiss immigrant Lorenz Enderle opened his own brewery in 1864, in a location that is likely familiar to St. Cloud residents. The Enderle Brewery was located at 409 Sixth Avenue, along the Mississippi River, where St. Cloud Cathedral High School has an athletic field today. It averaged a production of more than 20 barrels a month by its second year, and its production surpassed 1,600 barrels a month in 1879. Enderle was briefly

Enderle Brewery, near the location of the present-day St. Cathedral High School athletic field. *Courtesy of the Stearns History Museum.*

jailed in 1870 for violating revenue laws; after paying a $200 fine, he was released, and newspaper records indicate that he hosted a party for his closest friends at the brewery. A band performed, and a four-horse sleigh was brought in, decorated with flags—that's certainly one way to celebrate being released from jail.

Enderle sold the brewery to a trio of business partners in 1884 for $10,000, and it became known as the Empire Brewing Co. One of the brewery's new owners was Wendelin Merz, who also represented St. Joseph in the state legislature. When Merz passed in 1893, his wife, Carolyn, took over the brewery for three years. Valentine Udermann then bought the brewery in 1896. Udermann sold the building to saloon owners in 1909, and the business was closed in 1916. St. Cloud Cathedral High School built an athletic field on the site in 1921, and the Crusaders have trained there for decades.

RICHMOND BREWERY

Like many of Central Minnesota's communities, Richmond was settled by German immigrants in the 1850s. According to a *St. Cloud Times* article, there's some debate over whether the town along the Sauk River was named after the surname of an early resident or a town surveyor. Because another Minnesota town had already been using the name Richmond, when today's Richmond was established in 1856, it was known as Torah by the postal service and railroad stations. The city's name was officially changed to Richmond in 1909.

While the town was still known as Torah, in 1864, a brewery was launched there, along the west bank of the Sauk River. It's the first recorded brewery in Central Minnesota and Stearns County to be located outside the city of St. Cloud. The brewery was opened by Claudius Weber, who had moved to the area as a newlywed with his wife, Barbara. His German immigrant father-in-law, John Meyer, was also a part-owner of the brewery. Meyer sold his shares after three years, and the brewery was closed in 1869, just five years after it had opened.

Richmond hasn't had a commercial brewery since the Weber Brewery closed; instead, the town's citizens have found amusement through other means. The city is a part of the ROCORI school district, and it rallies around its amateur baseball team, the Richmond Royals, in the Stearns County League.

Sauk Centre Brewery

Northwest of St. Cloud, there is a city that was built on the ten-mile-wide Big Sauk Lake. Sauk Centre is a storied lake town that is most famously known as the hometown of author Sinclair Lewis. Lewis died from alcoholism in Rome, but he was buried in Sauk Centre at Greenwood Cemetery. The town's public park on the Big Sauk Lake has since been named Sinclair Lewis Park, and it hosts town festivals and events.

The spot where Sinclair Lewis Park rests today once housed a Sauk Centre brewery, which used water from the Big Sauk Lake. The brewery was launched in 1865 by German immigrant George Gruber, who hailed from the Bavarian region of Germany. Gruber also co-founded the local Sauk Centre Catholic Church. Gruber formed and led a social drinking club called the Wooden Shoe Association that met at the Sauk Centre Brewery and Taproom. Gruber's excuse to gather in a group to drink beer was a promotion ahead of its time. Years later, during the craft beer revolution, breweries across the country used different mug clubs and insider programs to gather and drink beer in brewery taprooms.

In 1867, a nearby dam broke and caused flooding throughout the area. While some local businesses had serious flood damage, the brewery, fortunately, only suffered minimal damage due to its position on higher ground. Tax records show that Henry Diehl purchased the brewery in 1885. The brewery again changed hands three years later, but a fire broke out and destroyed the brewery on February 14, 1895. It was never rebuilt. Sauk Centre hasn't had a brewery since, but the location of Gruber's original brewery now serves as a community park.

The Original Sauk Rapids Brewery

While St. Cloud ultimately became the hub of Central Minnesota, it wasn't initially intended to be. The adjacent town of Sauk Rapids, which is located on the other side of the Mississippi River, was meant to be the epicenter of the new settlement. When Sauk Rapids was discovered, it was densely covered by oak, maple and basswood forests. Its location on the Mississippi River, in the center of the Minnesota Territory, made it an ideal spot for settlement. Some legends even say Sauk Rapids was in the running to become Minnesota's capital due to its central location. The town was first settled in 1851, but it experienced a major tragedy on April 14, 1886. City records state that a devastating tornado demolished the heart of the city. The tornado killed forty-four and wounded several hundred other Sauk Rapids residents.

After the tornado, St. Cloud, on the other side of the Mississippi River, became the epicenter of Central Minnesota, as many former Sauk Rapids residents moved to St. Cloud. Much of the damage in Sauk Rapids was never repaired, but two years after the tornado, Adam Jocem opened the Sauk Rapids Brewing Co. The operation was also called Eagle Brewing but burned down on February 14, 1895; it was never rebuilt. And for more than a century, Eagle Brewing was the only brewery to ever operate in Benton County.

The Original St. Joseph Brewery

St. Joseph has always been known for its ties to the Catholic Church. The town, which is located less than ten miles west of St. Cloud, was originally named Clinton but was changed to St. Joseph, the name of the town's church, in 1870. For more than a century, St. Joseph has housed St. Benedict's Monastery and the College of St. Benedict, and the century-old St. John's Abbey and St. John's University is located nearby.

Louis Brinks founded a brewery in St. Joseph in 1870, and he used a Dutch-style windmill to grind the grain he needed for brewing. Brinks, however, was later arrested for illegally distilling liquor in November 1872. Brinks sold the St. Joseph Brewery in 1875 and ran another brewery in Frazee City until 1879. Then, in 1881, the St. Joseph Brewery burned down and was never rebuilt. Despite the fact that monks played integral roles in the overall history of brewing, there's no record of St. John's monks participating in any brewing—distilling, however, has a different story. St. John's and St. Benedict's have also long been known for their ancient Johnnie and Bennie bread recipes.

2

THE RISE AND FALL OF BREWING EMPIRES

While many of Central Minnesota's early breweries were short-lived, others prospered for decades and across multiple generations. The St. Cloud Brewing Company, Little Falls' Kiewel Brewery and New Munich's Pitzl Brewery all were thriving in the days before Prohibition. Old Heidelberger and Weiner Lager Beer became the first popular beers in Central Minnesota. The dry era of Prohibition in America, however, caused some of Central Minnesota's breweries to change course in what they produced, and it caused the complete end of other operations. While it was illegal at the time, alcohol was continually produced in Central Minnesota throughout Prohibition.

Moonshine production became central to the survival of Stearns County farmers during the Great Depression. In 2007, late St. Cloud State University professor Elaine Young wrote a phenomenal book about this era called *Minnesota 13: Stearns County's Wet Wild Prohibition Days*; the book has since been turned into a documentary. According to Davis's research, the monks of St. John's Abbey ran one of the largest and most profitable stills in Stearns County. Federal agents reportedly came to bust up the still, but the monks had returned to praying by the time they arrived. Central Minnesota's bootlegging production was so big that American gangster Al Capone visited the area. Although it was illegal, the popular opinion among Stearns County residents was that making alcohol was not immoral.

Because it was more efficient to make moonshine, Davis pointed out that it is likely very little beer was made during Prohibition. However, the laws still didn't stop one of Central Minnesota's most legendary breweries from brewing beer. The brewery's defiance ended in a bone-bruising brawl during a raid of federal agents.

The following are the brewing empires of Central Minnesota that rose and fell in the days before and after Prohibition.

St. Cloud Brewing Company

A large granite stone rests at the intersection of Seventh Street and Eighth Avenue in St. Cloud. It's the last remnant of the St. Cloud Brewing Company—a giant, yellow-brick brewery that operated there for decades. Longtime St. Cloud residents will also remember the space as the Purity Milk Company, which occupied the space for several decades after the brewery closed.

The genesis of the St. Cloud Brewing Company building started in 1869, when Fritz Herberger opened his own brewery there. He was a member of the Herberger family that later opened the once-thriving Herberger's Retail Store. Fritz's brother Judd became a co-owner of the brewery in 1874, and it became known as Herberger Brothers Brewery. The Herbergers sold the brewery in 1877 in order to open their own vinegar factory. The new owner of the brewery was a twenty-five-year-old Canadian named John Brick. The brewery had a bar and hotel attached, and Brick advertised it in the German-language newspaper *Nordstern*.

His brewery was successful, and by 1880, it led all of St. Cloud's breweries, which collectively ranked fourth in the state in beer production, trailing only St. Paul, Minneapolis and Stillwater. Tax records indicate that Central Minnesota's breweries collectively produced more than six thousand barrels of beer in 1880, when the number of breweries in Minnesota peaked before Prohibition, with 132 locations. Brick became well known throughout the community; in fact, historians say that Brick was so well liked that his 1886 funeral was the largest in the city's history at that point. Two years before Brick passed away, he sold the brewery to two business partners, Andrew Preiss and John Wimmer, who took the brewery to an even higher level.

Preiss and Wimmer took over the brewery in 1884. Their last names are included on the commemorative stone that was placed on the site more than a century later. The duo is considered to have been the most successful St. Cloud brewers before Prohibition. Preiss was born in Bayern, Germany, in

The old Preiss & Wimmer Brewing Co. in St. Cloud. The facility was also known as the St. Cloud Brewing Company *Courtesy of the Stearns History Museum.*

the Bavarian region, in 1853. Before he arrived in St. Cloud to take over the brewery, Preiss had worked in breweries throughout the Midwest, in Milwaukee, Wisconsin; Davenport, Iowa; and Perham, Minnesota. Preiss was a skilled brewer, and the public took notice. He ran the production side of the brewery, while Wimmer ran the business side. Wimmer was also a member of St. Cloud's city council.

Preiss and Wimmer continued to scale up their production. They made a significant financial investment to improve their facility in 1898. By 1900, when a sixteen-ounce pint cost only a nickel, the brewery had increased its production to ten thousand barrels annually. Preiss and Wimmer made more investments in the brewery in 1907 and 1909, including a new bottling line that they purchased from Chicago. Preiss and Wimmer also created the St. Cloud Brewing Company's most trademarked beer in 1909. The duo opened up the naming of the beer to the public; more than three thousand submissions were made at time when St. Cloud only had about ten thousand total residents. The winning entry for the lager's name was "Old Heidelberger," which referenced an old German castle. Lifelong St. Cloud resident Joseph Materna, who later served in World War I, submitted the winning entry and was rewarded with twenty-five dollars—although he was mistakenly called Joseph Martini in a *St. Cloud Times* report about the beer. Old Heidelberger became St. Cloud's flagship beer for years to come, and it is one of the most iconic brands in St. Cloud's brewing history. Ironically, another trademark St. Cloud craft beer was named by a public contest more than a century later.

Despite the success of Old Heidelberger, the business side of the St. Cloud Brewery struggled as Prohibition loomed. The St. Cloud Brewing Company declared bankruptcy in 1916 and went into receivership. At the onset of Prohibition, the brewery was purchased by former Jacob Schmidt Brewing Co. brewer John Nicolin. He converted the operation's production to brewing soft drinks and near beer, which had under .5 percent alcohol, in order to keep the business afloat during Prohibition.

When Prohibition was repealed, St. Cloud Brewing Company was issued a permit to brew beer in April 1933. Bavarian-born Ernst Weiss was hired as a brewmaster, and the brewery resumed its production of Old Heidelberger (many labels from this era are still found by collectors). While alcohol returned to the market after Prohibition, there were still many restrictions on the production of alcohol that had not existed before the nationwide ban. These restrictions made operating a financially successful brewery more complicated, and once again, the St. Cloud Brewing Company went into receivership in 1937. The brewery was closed two years later, in 1939.

The building became the home of the since-closed Purity Milk Company, which employed St. Cloud residents for decades. The actual St. Cloud Brewing building was demolished in 1986, and an apartment complex sits on the site today. Many future brewing operations contemplated reviving the St. Cloud Brewing name but ultimately picked different paths. The commemorative stone is the last remnant of the St. Cloud Brewing empire that once stood on the site.

Brewing in Little Falls

The Mississippi River pauses in a majestic spot on the northern edge of Central Minnesota. The slate and granite waterfalls in this location were dubbed "Little Falls" by the area's European settlers when they first arrived in the mid-1800s. According to Little Falls city records, the waterfall had numerous names and descriptions before it was named by the Europeans. Previously, the Ojibwa Native American tribe had called it *KaKaBikans*, which loosely translates to "little squarely rock." Native tribes used the area to collect resources. New Jersey–born explorer Zebulon Pike documented his 1805 quest through the area and described the Little Falls as "a remarkable rapid in the river, opposite a high piney island." French explorer Joseph Nicollet called the falls *Petite Chutes* in 1837. Other early visitors to Little Falls included fur traders and missionaries.

The Little Falls Mills and Land Company was formed in 1849 to build a dam, the first of four built in Little Falls. It was constructed in 1887 and brought a number of businesses and people to the area. The falls that had previously attracted the attention of natives and explorers alike were now powering a growing city that would later be the birthplace and hometown of American icon and aviator Charles Lindbergh.

People began using the water from Little Falls to brew beer in 1882. Leo Brick opened a brewery at 508 Seventh Street Northeast, and the operation became known as the Little Falls Brewing Co. in 1884. The company changed hands multiple times until 1893, when it was purchased by Jacob Kiewel. During the previous fall, Kiewel's popular Fergus Falls Brewery had burned down, and there was no sense in him rebuilding there, as Otter Tail County was in the process of becoming dry. So, Kiewel purchased the Little Falls brewery for $15,000 in May 1893. The brewery's previous owner, R.J. Koch, was selling in order to open another brewery in Ohio. Kiewel immediately updated the brewery and built a bottling house and new cellars. The brewery's new beers included White Seal, White Label, Grain Lager and White Rose. Kiewel added to his empire in 1899, when he bought the Crookston Brewing Co. The brewing operation became one of the largest in the state.

Kiewel adapted when Prohibition hit in 1920. The brewery was renamed Kiewel Associated Products and became a creamery that produced products like condensed milk, ice cream and butter. When Kiewel died in 1928, his son Joseph took over Kiewel Associated Products and led the company's resumption of producing beer after Prohibition. Joseph served as Kiewel Brewing's head brewer until 1952. Kiewel was one of Minnesota's last independent breweries when it sold to Grain Belt in 1959. The beer industry had changed drastically in the post-Prohibition world, as fewer breweries took much larger shares of the sales market. The price of beer became the ultimate purchasing factor for beer drinkers, so larger operations had an advantage over independent breweries.

Grain Belt had been launched in Minneapolis in 1893 and was one of the few beers to still be served more than one hundred years later. It is still produced today, after the brand was saved by New Ulm's August Schell's Brewing Co. in 2002. Grain Belt operated the old Little Falls Kiewel Brewery for just two years before closing it in 1961. Morrison County wouldn't host another brewery for nearly six decades. The old Kiewel Brewery building was purchased by the City of Little Falls in 1982 and was demolished the following year. Years later, beer was once again created with the water of the Mississippi River in Little Falls with the craft beer emergence.

Breweries and Brawls in New Munich

The town of New Munich is a Central Minnesota spot that could be easily missed if you blink. The Stearns County town is about thirty miles northwest of St. Cloud and has never had more than a couple hundred residents. New Munich was incorporated in 1856 and later housed a Soo Line train station. The town was named after one of its first settlers, a hunter who emigrated from Munich, Germany. Minnesota's Bavarian counterpart is much larger, with well over one million residents. It's hard to believe that Minnesota's third-largest brewery was once operated in a town that was mentioned in *Lake Wobegon Stories* and was home to an amateur baseball team called the Silverstreaks.

New Munich's history in brewing began in 1868, when John Froehler launched a brewery with his sons along the Sauk River, at the intersection of Main Street and Seventh Avenue. In 1889, the Froehler family hired a Hungarian immigrant named Mathew Pitzl, who later transformed the brewery and led it to its peak production. Originally, Pitzl was the personal driver of the Froehler family, but he was eventually trained to someday take over the brewery. Pitzl later apprenticed at St. Paul's Shelby Brewery before he returned to New Munich in 1900, purchasing the brewery from the Froehler family for $5,500. After this, the brewery quickly became known as Pitzl Brewing, and its upgrades included new iron sill girders, cement floors and modern machinery. Pitzl quickly increased the brewery's production from thirteen barrels a month to eight hundred a month. The brewery's signature brew was called Weiner Lager Beer. By 1910, Pitzl had turned his brewery into the largest in Stearns County. The brewery's total

The Pitzl Brewing Co. in the small Stearns County town of New Munich in 1900. The brewery became one of Minnesota's largest before Prohibition and was known for its signature brew called Weiner Lager. *Courtesy of the Stearns History Museum.*

production ranked third in the state, as Weiner Lager Beer was being more widely distributed. The little town of New Munich had one of Minnesota's most successful breweries.

Pitzl's empire was running smoothly until Prohibition took effect in 1920. Pitzl continued brewing and sold his products more discreetly. However, the New Munich brewery was raided by federal agents in 1924, and its remaining beer products were destroyed. Pitzl was charged with illegally selling beer, but he went down swinging. Records say that federal Prohibition agent Albert Whitney suffered a fractured skull at the hands of Pitzl during the raid of the New Munich brewery.

In 1927, Pitzl sought to start brewing legally again, so he packed up his brewing equipment and moved to Canada. Pitzl Brewing was moved to Estevan, Saskatchewan, Canada, on a fourteen-car Soo Line train. Pitzl planned to continue making Weiner Lager Beer after establishing a new Canadian beer empire, but his Canadian version of Pitzl Brewing ended up being a failure. Unlike the Sauk River water in New Munich, the water in Estevan was contaminated with alkali salts, so Pitzl could not make the beer to his standards.

Pitzl died in Canada in 1931, and his remains were returned to New Munich for a funeral. The attempts to resurrect the New Munich brewery after Prohibition in 1933 and 1953 ultimately failed. An old, eighteen-foot-deep cistern well from the brewery was sealed in February 2008 as part of a Minnesota Department of Health project that cost more than $6,000. In a press release about the project, inspector Keith Donabauer called the well the most dangerous cistern well he'd ever seen. The brewery was torn down soon thereafter—so little remains of New Munich's past brewing empire.

Melrose and the Sweetheart Beer Saga

Pomp and circumstance accompanied the laying of the cement at Schatz-Brau Brewing Co. in October 1933. Schatz-Brau Brewing, the Melrose brewery named for the German words for "Sweetheart Beer," was planned to open on the north side of the Sauk River Dam. A German band performed, a boxing match was hosted, a free movie was offered to the 1,500 attending

The Melrose brewery near the Sauk River Dam in 1933. The facility was a New Deal project that came with a town celebration after Prohibition was repealed. *Courtesy of the Stearns History Museum.*

and an evening dance with a ten-cent cover charge was held from 8:00 p.m. to just before midnight. Schatz-Brau had received funding from President Franklin Delano Roosevelt's New Deal program. Local politicians from both major political parties supported the project, which aimed to revitalize Melrose's economy and workforce. The mood at the concrete-laying party was certainly celebratory.

Melrose had supported a successful brewery prior to Prohibition. The town was settled in 1857 and organized in 1866; the town was named by early resident Warren Adley, in honor of his daughters Melissa and Rose. John Schnitz started the first Melrose brewery in 1882, along the Sauk River. The brewery was taken over by other owners in 1883 and 1884. It eventually became known as the Melrose Brewing Co. and produced a trademarked beer called the Old Bohemian Beer. German immigrants Andrew and Peter Stalboerger eventually took over the operations of the brewery. About a decade before Prohibition, the Melrose Brewing Co. had almost doubled its production to more than three thousand barrels annually. Unfortunately, a fire burned down the Melrose Brewing Co. in 1914. Newspaper archives say that the fire caused $50,000 worth of damage. The Melrose Brewing Co. was rebuilt and reopened but was ultimately closed in 1916, just two years after the fire.

Schatz-Brau was meant to revive Melrose's past brewing culture, and the brewery did a lot to generate hype for its opening. But despite all of the fanfare, Schatz-Brau never actually brewed any beer. The facility was converted into a cheese factory, instead of a brewery, before it was opened to the public. Schatz-Brau forever rests as a lost beer of Central Minnesota.

3

COLD SPRING BREWING EMERGES

A German immigrant named Michael Sargl set up a brewery in 1874 at a site in Cold Spring that he labeled "Pure Spring Waters." More than 130 years later, Sargl's creation is remarkably still standing and brewing. The Cold Spring Brewing Company operates on the very spot that Sargl built his brewery. Cold Spring Brewing only trails New Ulm's August Schell's Brewing Co., which was launched in 1860, on the list of Minnesota's oldest operating breweries. This operation has survived numerous reincarnations and owners, Prohibition and several financial issues. Sargl called his fermented creation "Bright Beer," and he used a large kettle in his brewing process.

The Cold Spring Creek was used as the brewery's source of water, as its water was high quality and fed in by a glacial lake. Sargl was an expert in wells and sought to imitate the storied German breweries of his home country. Cold Spring has been identified by its storied brewery ever since it opened. The city has three properties in the National Register of Historic Places, and they all belonged to people who ran the brewery.

After Bright Beer came Cold Spring Export, a Billy Beer made in conjunction with then-president Jimmy Carter's brother; the personal brand of the Hollywood horror character Elvira; the brief revival of Minnesota's storied Glueck brand; and the craft beers made under the Third Street Brewhouse label today. Cold Spring also uses its current state-of-the-art brewhouse to make contract brews for other craft breweries and has become one of the nation's largest producers of energy drinks.

Tradition is a big part of the culture in Cold Spring, even outside of the centuries-old brewery. A granite company and a Gold 'n Plump Poultry plant have also been longtime employers in the area. The Cold Spring Bakery, which has operated since 1946, is one of the most revered establishments in Central Minnesota; in 2013, it even opened a second storefront in Waite Park due to popular demand. The area of Cold Spring was visited by early fur trappers maneuvering up the Sauk River. A Native American trading post was established near the Red River in 1852, and German Catholic settlers arrived in the area in 1855. The area was named Cold Spring City the following year; "City" was dropped from the name in 1889, following a town petition.

During summer months, the residents of Cold Spring would pack the town's baseball stadium every week to watch its amateur baseball team, the Cold Spring Springers, play. The ROCORI (Rockville, Cold Spring and Richmond) High School's Spartans teams have also won multiple state titles. Former NFL receiver Eric Decker grew up in the city, and he first played at the University of Minnesota before he was drafted by the Broncos. Decker also played for the Jets, Titans and Patriots. When Decker was a student at ROCORI, he was present for the school's biggest tragedy. ROCORI was the site of a 2003 school shooting, just four years after the Columbine High School massacre. A freshman named Jason McLaughlin shot and killed fifteen-year-old freshman Seth Bartell and seventeen-year-old senior Aaron Rollins. McLaughlin was arrested and has been imprisoned ever since. Another tragedy occurred in Cold Spring in November 2012, when thirty-one-year-old Cold Spring–Richmond police officer Tom Decker was shot and killed in the line of duty in downtown Cold Spring. He was surprisingly not related to Eric Decker, but he was remembered through the renaming of the post office and a strip of Minnesota Highway 23 after him.

Like the community of Cold Spring, Cold Spring Brewing Company has faced its share of adversity. Its final chapter has nearly been written multiple times, but it has persevered as a significant part of Minnesota's brewing history.

EARLY COLD SPRING BREWING HISTORY

While Sargl's creation is still standing, well over a century after he first brewed there, his tenure with the brewery only lasted a few years. John Ladner took

The Cold Spring Brewing Company in 1906. *Courtesy of the Stearns History Museum.*

over as the brewery's second owner, and Jacob Haeman succeeded him as the third owner in 1884. Six years later, Haeman married Rose Friedmann of Cold Spring and added a brewery partner who would change the course of the operation.

John Oster joined Haeman in the business in 1890, because he had a broken piece of farm equipment that was rigged to work in the brewing process. Oster had a steam engine thresher that was fueled by cordwood. When a separator was worn out, Oster would use this machine, instead, to grind beer mash. Haeman had previously used horses to move a wheel treadmill that was attached to a pulley with a belt to turn the two rollers and grind the barley. This new equipment, however, was much more efficient. Along with the machine, Oster invested cash into the business.

Oster had been inspired to attempt bottling beer; at the time, the brewery, and many like it, just kegged its beer. Shortly after becoming a co-owner, Oster attempted to create a bottling house for the brewery. Everything was done by hand. Bottles were first washed and filled, one at a time; then, labels were individually placed by workers, who then finished the process by snap-capping the top of the bottle. It's a far cry from the highly automated process of bottling today, which is done in minutes. The bottling house employed a half dozen workers, who bottled beer for ten hours a day, six days a week. Oster's vision, however, turned out to be a bit too aggressive of a gamble for the time period. The original bottling plan was quickly discontinued, as the brewery lacked the equipment and money it needed to build a proper production line.

While his bottling line had failed, Oster brought plenty of success to Cold Spring Brewing. Five years after he became a co-owner, the brewery produced one thousand barrels of beer in a year for the first time. And in 1895, Haeman sold his share of the brewery to Henry Hilt, who became Oster's brewery partner. Hilt's tenure with the brewery was shortened, however, by hay fever. He left for Washington to focus on improving his health. Hilt eventually returned to Cold Spring and the brewery, but his fever relapsed, and he once again left for Washington. Before he left, Hilt asked his relative Ferdinand Peters to take his place at the brewery. Peters was born in Wisconsin and had prior brewing experience working for the Minneapolis Brewing Co.

From all indications, Oster and Peters hit it off immediately. Together, they brought in an experienced brewmaster from Wadena, Minnesota, named Eugene Hermanutz to run the brewery's production. Hermanutz immigrated to Minnesota from Germany in 1896. While in Germany, he had apprenticed with a brewmaster from a young age. Oster and Peters liked his beer formulas so much that they gave him stock ownership in the brewery. The operation was formally incorporated as the Cold Spring Brewing Company in 1900. Previously, the brewery had been registered under the last name of whoever the owner was at the time. The Cold Spring Brewing Company was born under a trio of leadership: Oster as the president and general manager; Hermanutz as the vice president and head brewer; and Peters as the secretary-treasurer.

The Cold Spring Brewing Company operated out of a two-story building; the first level was used for offices, and the second level—while it was initially used to house single employees—was later used to make and repair wooden barrels and cases. Water from the same creek that Sargl had first tapped into was being piped into the brewery through the cement floor. The brewery's compound also included a barn that housed eighteen horses that were used for beer delivery; Oster and Peters also traveled by horse to saloons, where they collected bills, became acquainted with patrons and offered samples. Salesmen of cigars, cigarettes, candy and nuts often followed behind the Oster and Peters convoy, finding easy sales among tipsy patrons. The Cold Spring Brewing Company's production peaked at twenty-five thousand barrels a year before Prohibition.

The Cold Spring Brewing Company eventually diversified its production and began making soft drinks in addition to beer—something the operation has done ever since. It also started selling distilled water sold to hospitals, homes, cafés, restaurants and moonshiners. The Cold Spring Mineral Water Company was formed and found popularity in the dry counties of Minnesota and South Dakota. The brand Red Star Mineral Water helped put Cold Spring on the map, and it kept Cold Spring Brewing Company afloat when Prohibition hit in 1920. The mineral water company lasted until 1933.

Oster and Peters also diversified their interests during Prohibition by investing in the Cold Spring Granite Co. in 1920. They both went on to serve as Cold Spring's mayor, as would Oster's sons, Dan and Ed. Oster's 201 North Red River Avenue home was built in 1907, Peters's 214 North Red River Avenue home was built in 1907 and Hermanutz's 302 North Red River Avenue home was built in 1912. The neighboring homes sit across the street from the brewery and were each added to the National Register of Historic Places in 1982.

Oster died on September 10, 1930, after working at the brewery for more than forty years. While he never realized his dream of opening a fully functioning bottling plant, his vision soon became a reality and brought Cold Spring Brewing Company back from the brink after Prohibition.

4

COLD SPRING BREWING RETURNS AFTER PROHIBITION

After the passage of Prohibition, federal agents raided the Cold Spring Brewery and dumped its remaining products into the same creek that Michael Sargl had first used to brew his Bright Beer. Records say that brewer Eugene Hermanutz was too emotionally distraught to watch—decades later, his actions inspired the creation of another Cold Spring beer called Brewer's Tears.

Cold Spring Brewing Company was able to survive Prohibition by emphasizing its mineral water, and this wasn't the last time that soft drinks kept the business afloat. Cold Spring also made near beer that was less than .5 percent alcohol. When Prohibition was repealed, the brewery planned to revive its beer-making business. It ultimately became one of few Central Minnesota breweries that thrived both before and after Prohibition.

On April 7, 1933, a federal agent unlocked the padlock that had previously been placed on the doors of the Cold Spring Brewing Company. Guns were fired, and truck horns, sirens and church bells were sounded off in celebration. A thirty-four-truck convoy headed out of the brewery, carrying post-Prohibition beer. By 12:35 a.m., St. Cloud bars were back to serving Cold Spring Brewing Company beer. A longtime Cold Spring Brewing employee described the moment for a Stearns History Museum exhibit, saying, "[It was like] Christmas, New Year's Eve and everybody's birthday all rolled into one." Cold Spring Brewing was back in business.

Shortly after it returned to the market, the Cold Spring Brewery was robbed; its vault door was blasted off with nitroglycerin around 4:00 a.m. on April 15, 1933. The brewery put out an advertisement in the newspaper,

St. Stephen Mission Group members drinking Cold Spring Brewing beer in 1949. *Courtesy of the Stearns History Museum.*

offering a $200 reward for help in catching the robbers. They had taken securities, negotiable gold bonds, $750 in U.S. Revenue stamps, petty cash and an old coin collection—which included a gold coin that showcased a former German kaiser and an English coin from the Victorian era. Brewer Carl Geisner was working at the time of the blast but reportedly never saw any perpetrators. Some papers from the vault were eventually found on an Anoka riverbank (Anoka is another Minnesota city about sixty miles from Cold Spring), but there are no records that indicate the robbers were ever caught or identified.

The brewery's co-owner Ferdinand Peters died in 1938, and his son, Ferdinand Peters Jr., eventually followed his footsteps and became the head brewer. In the same year, Cold Spring experienced its last horse-drawn delivery of beer. Days after the attack on Pearl Harbor on December 7, 1941, Peters Jr. was inspired to sign up to fight in World War II—a new person was needed to manage the business.

Cold Spring Brewing's owners then turned to a Minneapolis Coca-Cola employee named Myron Johnson. The University of Minnesota and College of St. Thomas alumnus had studied finance and management, and he had been part of Coca-Cola's management training. While he was a student, Johnson often held multiple jobs. He was born in Wausau, Wisconsin, to an Italian-German mother and a Norwegian father. Johnson was always a bit smaller than other boys his age, but he was ferocious enough to play both hockey and football for the College of St. Thomas. After graduation, he used that scrappiness to his advantage in the business world.

When Johnson was hired at Cold Spring Brewing, he brought a new approach to the business. At the time of Johnson's hiring, the brewery had been producing around seven thousand barrels of beer a year. And although many of the brewery's employees had been skeptical of Johnson's hiring at first—initially talking in German behind his back—they eventually came to trust him, and he became the undisputed face of Cold Spring Brewing for several decades. Good sanitation was something he demanded. "The first thing he did was close it to clean it up," said Johnson's son, Tom, in an interview with the *St. Cloud Times*. "It was not Coca-Cola clean, and that's where he was from, and that's how it was going to be."

Johnson also had to deal with the challenge of operating a business during World War II. He took numerous trips to Washington, D.C., to lobby the ration board for supplies. After two years as an executive member of the brewery's board, Johnson purchased ownership; the natural entrepreneur had fallen in love with the beer business. Johnson later served on the president's council of the College of St. Benedict, as the director of the Minnesota Bowler's Association and as the president of the Minnesota Bowling Council. He was also a member of an Elks Lodge, the Knights of Columbus and the Serra and St. Cloud Country Clubs. Johnson also served on the board of the United States Brewers Association, one of the precursors to the current Brewers Association.

While Johnson had many accomplishments to his credit, he wasn't a professional brewer, so he hired Fred Hoerber as his senior master brewer in 1945. The fourth-generation brewmaster grew up in Chicago, where his parents ran a brewery. Hoerber also apprenticed at a number of other Chicago breweries before he graduated from the Siebel Institute in 1936. He attended Carleton College in Northfield, Minnesota, and Northwestern University in Evanston, Illinois. Prior to his several-decade-long stint at Cold Spring Brewing, Hoerber served as the brewmaster at the Tropical Brewing Co. in Puerto Rico.

Roman DeWenter also served as a key employee of Cold Spring Brewing for numerous decades. He was born in a small town west of Cold Spring and St. Cloud called Sedan, Minnesota—it had a recorded population of forty-five people in the 2010 census—but he was raised in Cold Spring. He was initially hired as a bookkeeper at Cold Spring Brewing Company when it first reopened after Prohibition. At the time, DeWenter had just graduated from St. Cloud Business College. He went on to fill a variety of roles at the brewery before he ended his career as the brewery's president. He was also an active member of the community, running the local Boy Scouts program and serving as a chief ranger of the Catholic Order of Foresters. DeWenter was also a member of the local Lions, a sportsman and chamber of commerce club. Together, DeWenter and his wife, Ethel, had six children.

Johnson made a continual effort to improve Cold Spring Brewing. He was constantly investing in the facility, renovating and modernizing its production process. As other breweries struggled to exist in the post-Prohibition era, Cold Spring Brewing often purchased their pieces of used equipment at a discount. Myron also began purchasing other brewery brands, like Mankato Brewing and Gluek Brewing, which was acquired by Cold Spring in 1971 but not used until decades later. A Mankato Brewing employee named Jim Schorn was hired by Cold Spring and worked there for several decades.

Cold Spring Brewing had increased its production to thirty-five thousand barrels a year by 1966, and it had about thirty wholesalers at the time. A few years later, the brewery received an investment of $600,000. The brewery then started producing Kegle Brau, Arrowhead and a beer that was made with a University of Minnesota–developed hybrid corn variety called Minnesota 13. Its production surpassed fifty-two thousand barrels a year in 1971.

While Cold Spring Brewing found ways to survive and continually increase its production, the rest of Minnesota's brewery scene struggled to exist. By 1976, Cold Spring Brewing was 1 of only 4 breweries left operating in the state, alongside August Schell in New Ulm and Schmidt Brewing and Stroh Brewing Co. in St. Paul. This downturn in the number of Minnesota breweries came nearly a century after the state had reached its pre-Prohibition peak of 132 total breweries. Clearly, the beer industry had reached a new era. "In this industry, you either get larger or you die," said Tom Johnson in an interview with the *St. Cloud Times*. "It's the quick and the dead. If you're static, you are losing ground." In July 1978, the thirty-person Cold Spring Brewing staff went on a ten-day strike. "A strike is never pleasant," Tom Johnson said. "You have outside factions coming in and stirring people up who you would like to think are your friends. It can be pretty tough." The strike was resolved when workers were given a 27 to 30 percent raise, about $1.10 at the time. At the same time, a new beer idea was brewing that would give Cold Spring Brewing Company national recognition.

Billy Beer

An opportunity to gain national headlines soon presented itself to the Cold Spring Brewing Company, when it was asked to contract brew Billy Beer, the personal brand for then-president Jimmy Carter's eccentric brother, Billy Carter. The gas station proprietor and farmer had been labeled as a "professional redneck" by the Associated Press. Some quotes from Billy Carter include, "I got a red neck, white socks and Blue Ribbon beer."

Falls City Brewing Company, based in Louisville, Kentucky, saw Billy Carter as an opportunity to cash in on a novelty brand. Jimmy Carter had been sworn in as president earlier in 1977. The brewery agreed to a licensing deal with Billy and began giving him different beer recipes to try. Billy pledged to become the "Colonel Sanders of beer." Falls City contracted Cold Spring, Texas's Pearl Brewing and New York's West End Brewing to produce and can Billy Beer. Republican state representative Gary Laidig unsuccessfully tried to stop the release of Billy Beer by arguing against celebrity endorsements of alcohol. The publicity for Billy Beer began to spread, and rumors swirled that Billy Carter would visit Cold Spring to promote the beer. Billy Beer was a lager brewed with an imported German yeast, and its production took about eleven weeks. Plant superintendent Myron Mosell commented to the *St. Cloud Times* just before the beer's release, "We're a little edgy. We want to make sure everything is right."

The first one hundred thousand cases of the orange, white and blue cans of beer were trucked out of the Cold Spring Brewery on November 11, 1977. The six-packs were sold for two dollars each, and every label included Billy's signature and his motto: "I had this beer brewed up just for me. I think it's the best I ever tasted. And I've tasted a lot. I think you'll like it, too." A convoy of fifty-two trucks lined up for the first delivery out of Cold Spring, which was to be shipped throughout Minnesota and Wisconsin. Community members lined Cold Spring's streets as the convoy left the brewery—some pedestrians even toasted beers to the honking truck drivers as they passed by. Myron compared the Billy Beer release to a circus when he spoke to reporters. State senator Ed Schrom and Cold Spring mayor Pat Cheeley attended the ceremony, but there was no appearance of Carter himself.

Cold Spring Brewing, again, teased a potential Billy Carter visit in 1978. The brewery planned a "Peanut Derby," where teams would compete in peanut tosses, peanut butter eating contests and other peanut-themed games. Johnson publicly said that he planned to pay Carter more than $10,000 to make the two-day visit. However, his plans unfortunately fell through, and

A can of Billy Beer. The brew was made in honor of then-president Jimmy Carter's eccentric brother, Billy Carter, in 1977. *Courtesy of the Stearns History Museum.*

Carter never set foot in Cold Spring. According to the *L.A. Times*, Carter entered rehab for alcoholism a few years after the demise of Billy Beer. He died from pancreatic cancer at the age of fifty-one in 1988. Billy Beer cans remain popular, although not rare, among beer can collectors. "It was planned to be a flash in the pan kind of thing, and it was," said Tom Johnson to the *St. Cloud Times* decades later. "In Billy Carter's defense—because he was an odd guy—Billy did have a discerning palate when it came to beer. Practice makes perfect, because he liked to drink." Jimmy Carter, who served as president from 1977 to 1981, would also have a profound impact on the beer world when he deregulated homebrewing, spawning curious beer drinkers to make their own creations at home across the United States.

The late 1970s brought other new beers to Cold Spring Brewing aside from just Billy Beer. Cold Spring Export, which was modeled after malty imported beers like Heineken and Beck, was added to the brewery's production list in 1978. At this time, Cold Spring's mineral water line was also reinvigorated. New marketing promoted the Cold Spring product having less sodium than the established Perrier brand. In the 1980s, Johnson also made a marketing and distribution deal with G. Heileman Brewing of La Crosse, Wisconsin, to market Cold Spring Mineral Water.

Cold Spring's beer business began to drastically shrink during the 1980s. Johnson lobbied for small brewery tax credits as large commercial breweries began to dominate the industry. Cold Spring began to focus more heavily on its spring water and even halted its own beer production, just bottling and fermenting on site for contracted breweries, for multiple periods throughout the decade. Johnson was involved with the Cold Spring Brewing Company until his death on March 25, 1993. His family sold his former empire two years later, after its sales had plummeted 51 percent in just five years.

A company run by a former Adolph Coors executive called Pure Colorado agreed to purchase the 120-year-old brewery in 1995. The group was formed three years earlier and took on Cold Spring's debt from years of operating in the red. The brewery also needed to be refurbished, as it had outdated equipment. Pure Colorado was mostly interested in the mineral water portion of the business and planned to reformulate the brewery's flagship brands of Cold Spring and Cold Spring Light. In 1995, Cold Spring Brewing added a pale ale and red ale, and a year later, the brewery teamed with former Minnesota Twins Hall of Fame slugger Harmon Killebrew to make a nonalcoholic Killebrew brand of root beer.

Pure Colorado's owner, Tony Bottagaro, initially said all the right things; in an interview with the *Cold Spring Record* about the purchase, he said, "Cold Spring Brewery has been here for a long time. It's been through ups and downs, and we saw an opportunity to do some research and development. We see everything through optimistic eyes and see nothing but blue skies." But the debt that was owed by the brewery kept gray skies over the business. Pure Colorado, later renamed Beverage International, continued to struggle, and its attempts to register on the stock exchange as a public company failed. When brewery president Maurice Bryan called the headquarters of Beverage International in December 1996, he was surprised to learn that the business had closed and the executive team had walked away. The final checks that had arrived just before Christmas 1996 all bounced.

Cold Spring Brewing's assets were liquidated by Judge Bernard Boland in 1997, after the brewery defaulted on a $300,000 loan—far from the total debt that was owed. The brewery's other outstanding debts included $400,000 to Stearns County and $600,000 to its investor, Adar Securities. At that point, the brewery was in the possession of the First National Bank of Cold Spring. The company's century-old tradition of brewing beer in the same location in Cold Spring was in serious jeopardy. However, First National Bank's president, Glenn Heitzman, allowed the brewery to continue operations while a new buyer was sought—ultimately, he's the reason that Cold Spring Brewing is still operating today. Eventually, a local investment group, led by brewery executive Maurice Bryan, grocery store mogul Mabel Coborn and other investors in a group called Reflow Inc., stepped up to purchase the brewery in 1997.

Cold Spring Brewery was taken in a new direction by its new owners. It once again made a celebrity beer when it teamed up with the Hollywood horror character Elvira, played by actress Cassandra Peterson. Elvira had previously starred in a series of national Coors television advertisements, but when Coors dropped her as a spokesperson, she teamed up with Cold Spring Brewing to make Elvira's Night Brew. Former Cold Spring Brewing staff members compare the beer to Surly's Darkness. "It was a magnificent beer," recalled longtime Cold Spring Brewery employee Doug DeGeest to the *St.*

Cloud Times. "It was this big, wonderful malty beer. It was on the cutting edge of that time. If it existed now, it would probably be something popular." Unlike Billy Carter, Peterson traveled to Cold Spring as Elvira to promote her beer. "Cold Spring was fantastic," said Peterson in a phone interview with this book's author for the *St. Cloud Times*. "I remember coming when it was warm in the summer months. It was such a cool, old brewery. I was really impressed with it. It had this old, spooky vibe, which I love." Elvira's Night Brew also made national headlines for an incident at the 1997 Great American Beer Festival in Denver. Peterson had planned to promote the beer as the Elvira character but was barred from entering the festival for showing too much cleavage—although she claimed to any member of the Denver media who would listen that Peter Coors had ordered her banishment.

Cold Spring Brewing also resurrected the Gluek Brewing brand in 1997, as it had purchased the former brewery's recipe and branding decades before. Gluek was founded in 1857 by German immigrant Gottlieb Gluek in Northeast Minneapolis. The brewery had survived Prohibition and operated into the 1960s. Cold Spring bet on bringing the once-storied brand back, and it gained moderate popularity. A heavy rotation of radio advertisements during Minnesota Twins baseball broadcasts helped with the brand's notoriety, as the "Dazzle Man" Dan Gladden always spoke of his friends in Cold Spring. A pilsner, honey bock, ice lager and special light beer were all eventually released under the Gluek brand name. Cold Spring produced Gluek until 2010. The new owners of the brand have since resurrected the Gluek recipe in the Twin Cities.

One of the early partners in Reflow Inc. was John Lenore. The successful beverage and beer wholesaler started a California beverage empire in 1966, and he helped expand the soft drink business of Cold Spring Brewing. One of Lenore's contacts was the founder of what would become Monster Energy Drinks. Cold Spring Brewing has become one of the largest producers of energy drinks in the country since Lenore took leadership at the brewery. Lenore purchased the brewery from his Reflow Inc. partners in 2003, and he began investing millions into improving the facility. He soon built a state-of-the-art brewhouse, giving Cold Spring Brewing a new chapter and name for the craft beer revolution of the 2010s.

5

COLD SPRING'S NEW ERA

Third Street Brewhouse

Cold Spring Brewing's new owner, John Lenore, introduced a number of changes after taking over the storied business. The operation significantly increased its production of energy drinks, becoming one of America's largest energy drink plants. In 2008, the business began contract brewing for other breweries across the country, which has become a large source of revenue. The contract brewing business would, years later, grab national headlines for an unexpected reason; a Sacramento man named Brendan Peacock filed a 2018 false advertising lawsuit against the San Francisco Bay area's 21st Amendment Brewery for saying that their product was "Brewed and Canned by 21st Amendment Brewery, San Leandro, CA," when the beer was actually contract brewed at Cold Spring Brewing. Peacock later filed another lawsuit against PBR for marketing its beer as being made from "pure mountain water," when its water was actually sourced from the reservoirs of Los Angeles County.

While it was brewing other craft beer brands, Cold Spring Brewing began creating its own varieties to brew. Lenore planned to invest about $14 million into building a new brewhouse, and thanks to the Surly Bill that was passed the same year, a facility was opened in 2011 that included a taproom. People were soon able to enjoy pints at the Cold Spring Brewery; in previous years, state law had prohibited the existence of brewery taprooms, so Cold Spring had mainly focused on bar distribution.

At the time of the new brewhouse opening in 2011, beer preferences had evolved drastically. Hoppy beers that would have been far too bitter

The Third Street Brewhouse when it opened as the craft beer wing of the Cold Spring Brewing Company in 2011. *Courtesy of the Third Street Brewhouse.*

in previous generations soon became standard. While beer consumers had long valued price over quality, new taste buds caused new mentalities to form around beer. Cold Spring decided that it wanted to distance itself from its history of producing cheap beer, so it was now sold and packaged as Third Street Brewhouse—named after the intersecting street where the brewery has always stood. Longtime Cold Spring Brewing employee Doug DeGeest led the initial transformation, and a new canning line was added to complement the bottling line.

The name change brought plenty of confusion for consumers. Third Street employees often had to explain that they were a new wing of the Cold Spring Brewing Company and not a second Cold Spring craft brewery. Some of the brewery's neighbors also put up a stink about the new facility; at city council meetings, some complained of a residual odor from the brewery, the operation's water usage and the possibility of brown trout dying in a nearby stream. Third Street Brewhouse, however, was allowed to carry on with production and paid homage to its vocal detractors with its original flagship beers names: Bitter Neighbor black IPA and Lost Trout brown ale.

A new, experienced brewer was later hired to lead the new Third Street Brewhouse, and the brewmaster position, which had long been held by men of German heritage, was soon taken over by a man from Jamaica. DeGeest said he didn't think Jamaican-born Horace Cunningham would accept the job when he was offered the position. Cunningham had been with the Athens, Georgia brewery Terrapin Beer Co. directly prior to Third Street and had a long resume of brewing around the world. After earning an applied microbiology degree, Cunningham started making his native country's trademark Red Stripe lager at Desnoes & Geddes, a brewing company headquartered in Jamaica. He then moved on to brew beer in London and Barbados before he finally immigrated to Minnesota in 2001 to work at St. Paul's Summit Brewing Co., where he was employed for seven years. Cunningham also served as the second president of the Master Brewers Association of the Americas, which represented both North and South America. "Beer has brought me all over the world. And it continues to do so," said Cunningham in a *St. Cloud Times* profile. "It's been a long journey. It is more of a lifetime journey." Cunningham's original assistant at Third Street was also from the tropics; assistant brewmaster Steve Gittens was from Barbados and had also brewed all over the world.

Cunningham developed all of Third Street's inaugural brews. In addition to Bitter Neighbor and Lost Trout, he created a pale ale called Three Way and a cream ale called Rise to the Top. Cunningham also experimented with seasonal beers; Third Street Brewhouse partnered with the monks of St. John's Abbey to develop a maple stout called Sugar Shack. The beer was made with maple syrup that was tapped at the St. John's Abbey arboretum. Third Street also brewed a pale amber wheat ale called Hunny Do for spring and summer palates. Pumpkin spice was brewed into the fall seasonal beer called Jack'd Up. Coffee beans roasted locally by Mugsy's Beans were used in Third Street's popular imperial coffee porter called Cool Beans.

By 2014, Third Street had produced 28,237 barrels of beer. According to the Brewers Association, Third Street was the fourth-largest brewery in the state of Minnesota, but trouble was brewing in Cold Spring. An embezzlement scandal broke, and controller Adam Martin was eventually imprisoned for defrauding his employer, family and friends out of more than $680,000. Martin was convicted in 2017 and was given an eight- to ninety-six-month-long prison sentence. Tragedy struck Cold Spring again when owner John Lenore died in 2015. The brewery's ownership was transferred to the John Lenore Trust, which significantly cut back on its investment into the brewery. "I don't think people know how close we were to closing," former Cold Spring Brewing human resources manager Nicki Holthaus told St. Cloud Chamber of Commerce's *Business Central Magazine*. "We fine-tuned, worked on profitability, put in checks and balances, started an expansion and focused on community giving. We had three years to make ourselves profitable, and we did it."

Later in 2015, another major shakeup occurred at the brewery, when DeGeest, Cunningham and Gittens were suddenly relieved of their positions. Members of the brewery's talented sales staff bolted to positions elsewhere in the industry. The brewery's vice president of sales, Larry Williams, explained the changes as a "refocusing" to the *St. Cloud Times*. Third Street planned to pull some beers and add a new lager called Minnesota Gold, which they wanted to take nationwide with the tagline of "brewed in the land of 10,000 lakes." In order to make this plan successful, the Lenore Trust planned to utilize its distribution network. Along with all of this change, the Third Street Brewhouse's website was briefly hacked, along with several other businesses in the country, with messages claiming to be from the terrorist group ISIS. The FBI investigated the incident.

Third Street's new head brewer in 2015 was a familiar face and was one that would bring stability back to Cold Spring; Karl Schmitz had been with Third Street Brewhouse when the new facility had just opened, and he had spent several years with Cold Spring Brewing before then. He left Cold Spring to run West O Beer in Milford, Iowa, which is located just south of the Minnesota border, near Lake Okoboji. Schmitz honed his craft and recipe development, winning the 2014 and 2015 gold medals at the Great American Beer Festival for his chocolate stout. He was then recruited to come back home and lead the new era of Third Street. "I probably wouldn't have gone anywhere else," Schmitz told the *St. Cloud Times*. "I was very content where I was, but to come home is a big deal." Schmitz had grown up in Cold Spring, where he earned a job stacking pallets when he was eighteen years old. That gig led to a job working on the energy drink production side of the brewery in 2005. Schmitz, however, was curious about what went on in the brewery. When he had free time, he often wandered over to pick the brewers' minds. Schmitz was never a homebrewer, but he actually learned how to brew on Cold Spring's large scale when he was transferred over to the brewery.

Schmitz left Cold Spring in 2013 to run West O Beer, where he worked on a much smaller scale but learned more of the ins and outs of brewing. Schmitz also honed his recipe development—as his gold medals attest. Schmitz returned to Cold Spring after about three years. His first beer was a dry-hopped IPA called Hop Lift, which was made with six hundred pounds of hops per batch. He also released a light version of Minnesota Gold and a peach tree lager that has become a year-round beer. He's experimented with shandies, seltzers and a hazy brut. His session Oktoberfest and red ale, called Free Speech, have also become seasonal regulars. Lab technician Michael Gold moved his way up to serve under Schmitz as his lead brewer before he was promoted elsewhere in the company.

Schmitz has continued brewing many of Third Street's past beers—resurrecting some from decades ago. Inspiration for one came from an old file cabinet of former longtime brewer Mike Kneip. Schmitz swore that he searched through it previously in 2010 and didn't notice anything unique. But upon a second glance in 2017, he found a treasure-trove of handwritten, dated brewing notes folded up on the bottom of the folder. Most of the notes were written with German instructions and measurements. Old recipes for Cold Spring Pep and a bock were part of the collection. Schmitz also re-created one of the one-hundred-year-old recipes he found. The lager became known as Brewer's Tears, a throwback to former head brewer Eugene Hermanutz and his teary-eyed refusal to watch Cold Spring's last beer get dumped out at the start of Prohibition. While beers weren't known for their hop profiles in the past, this particular recipe had a malty lager base paired with mild bitterness. It was released in 2017, and Schmitz said that he plans to release other historic lagers.

Later, in 2017, a Greenwich, Connecticut equity firm company called Brynwood Partners VII purchased the Cold Spring Brewing Company from the Lenore family. At the time of the sale, Brynwood Partners VII announced in a press release that they had acquired a 350-employee business that had more than $60 million in net sales, annually, with the combined production of soft drinks and beers. The Brynwood Partners VII equity firm was formed in 1984 and said it had $725 million of private equity capital when it completed the Cold Spring purchase. Brynwood Partners VII already had a beverage empire before purchasing Cold Spring, as it had previously purchased the iconic Sunny Delight and Juicy Juice fruit drink brands under its Harvest Hill Beverage Co. label. The equity firm had also purchased Fairbault Foods, Inc.'s juice pouch manufacturing facility in Elk River and an energy drink brand from Nestlé prior to its Cold Spring acquisition. Brynwood Partners VII now holds the keys to the next chapters of the storied history of one of Minnesota's oldest breweries.

6
BREWPUBS BRING NEW BEER

In the days after Prohibition, the beer industry returned in the United States but became highly regulated. A new three-tiered system required the separation of manufacturers and retailers from independent distributors. This, in theory, limited any segment of the alcohol business from becoming too powerful, but it also meant breweries had to operate much differently than they had before. Breweries were initially barred from selling beer on their own premises; they were limited to providing free samples on tours or during special brewery events. The taverns and brewpubs that had long been a part of the European beer culture ceased to exist in the United States for several decades.

However, that all changed in the early 1980s, thanks to a European-born brewer who helped reintroduce the brewpub culture to America. In 1982, Scottish immigrant and brewing industry veteran Bert Grant helped change local laws and launched the first U.S. brewpub since Prohibition in Yakima, Washington, in an old opera house. Grant's Yakima Brewing & Malting Co. was later moved to a train depot, where it operated for several decades—Grant sold it 1995 and died in 2001. While the Yakima Brewing & Malting Co. was closed in 2006, its legacy looms large today, with brewpubs and taprooms being very much part of America's beer culture today. California's Mendocino Brewing Co. and Buffalo Bill's Brewpub followed Grant's lead by opening in 1983, and restrictive laws around the country began to be rewritten as brewpubs reemerged.

In Minnesota, Taps Waterfront Brewery and Comedy Club of Minneapolis was launched in 1989 as the state's first brewpub since Prohibition. The establishment would only operate for two years; *Land of Amber Waters* author Doug Hoverson wrote that Taps suffered from a poor location that had confusing parking options. But many imitators of the brewpub model soon emerged in the North Star State, taking advantage of the new deregulation paved by Taps.

St. Cloud played an essential role in the reemergence of brewpubs in the state. A storied St. Cloud restaurant called O'Hara's added a brewery to its location in 1996. It was far ahead of its time and helped build the state's coalition of craft breweries, inspired a new generation of homebrewers and future commercial brewers and was the launching point for one of Minnesota's most influential head brewers. Like many of the influential brewpubs before it, O'Hara's would close before the start of the most recent craft beer renaissance—which the brewery helped spark. Three years after O'Hara started brewing its own beers, Granite City Food & Brewery opened about a mile away, in St. Cloud, with its own brewpub. Granite City, which remains a popular St. Cloud eatery and watering hole today, eventually expanded throughout the country and has become a well-known national chain that bears the moniker of St. Cloud's city nickname in more than a dozen states.

O'Hara's Brewpub

O'Hara's had been operating as a bar and St. Cloud institution for five decades when its owner, Tim O'Hara, received a thank-you card in the mail that changed his life. The message was from former employee Shawn Gallus, who shared insight into the booming mid-1990s Colorado beer scene, particularly a brewpub in Fort Collins called CooperSmith's Pub & Brewing. After finding immediate success after its launch in 1989 and helping revitalize the city's downtown district, the founders of CooperSmith's—who included future Colorado governor John Hickenlooper—became consultants for similar operations around the country. CooperSmith's was set up in a town that had remained dry more than thirty years after Prohibition, but it launched a craft beer culture that now includes the iconic New Belgium Brewing, Odell Brewing and Funkwerks, among others.

O'Hara had hoped to do the same in Central Minnesota that CooperSmith's had done in Fort Collins. Beer had been the bulk of O'Hara's business at the time of Gallus's note—about 70 percent of all sales. Tim O'Hara figured it was a business trend worth trying, but it meant that the storied establishment, known for its Irish name, needed a new identity.

O'Hara's was opened in 1945 under the name Sid & Cecil's Little City. Tim's grandfather Sid O'Hara and uncle Cecil O'Hara had started the business together shortly after the end of World War II. The brothers, who grew up in Pembina, North Dakota, took over the location, which had previously housed Gus' Place, when its owner, Gus Anderson, died. Cecil had already been living in St. Cloud when the opportunity arose. Sid, meanwhile, took a $460 cab ride from Long Beach, California, to join his brother as partner in St. Cloud—a story he often repeated to friends and family. Sid & Cecil's was started as a bar that was restricted to serving beer that contained 3.2 percent alcohol. The establishment also operated as a grocery store and market that was frequented by the residents of a nearby trailer park. Sid quickly emerged as the leader of the operation. To get the business launched, the former navy baker worked every day from 8:00 a.m. to 1:00 a.m. for several months. Cecil shifted his focus to other business ventures, launching an off-sale liquor store and barbershop in Sid & Cecil's Little City. The O'Haras also rented out units in the trailer park, and the area became its own sub-community within St. Cloud.

Sid eventually added a small food menu to the bar. The restaurant's trademark became its hot beef sandwiches that were served on wax paper and filled with rump roast that had been slowly cooked with onions and bay leaves. The menu also offered a Polish sausage and different soups. Sid became a well-known local businessman and entrepreneur and later married Margaret "Dot" O'Hara. Sid joined the West Side Progressive Club in the 1950s and remained a member for about a decade; he also championed a number of military groups for veterans. And once, Sid even ran for city council. His family and friends often remark on Sid's innate ability to remember people's names—a trait that endeared him to a number of people. Sid was known to be sensitive toward people who had tough financial situations. He routinely forgave grocery store debt, delivered goods to needy families on holidays and hosted Christmas parties for the kids of the trailer park. During the Vietnam War, he even aided a grieving St. Cloud family that had lost their son in battle.

Sid retired in 1978 and sold the business to his sons, Tim and Mick. The brothers had grown up working at the family businesses, where they were assigned daily chores once they turned five. Tim eventually took sole possession of the business. While Sid had stopped running O'Hara's day-to-day business, he remained a fixture at the restaurant, working as a host during lunch. Sid also remained a regular diner, always nabbing the table near the kitchen and server stations known to staff as table no. 162. When O'Hara's started brewing its own beer, Sid latched onto its honey wheat variety and championed the homemade brews to guests. Dot died in 2000, and a year later, Sid passed away at the age of seventy-eight.

Tim and Mick transformed O'Hara's the moment they took over the family business from their father. They immediately constructed a new building to house their business, and the remodeled structure featured an expanded kitchen and menu additions, including burgers and other bar foods. The daily special rotated, with mashed potatoes always offered as the side dish to cater to the simplistic Midwest appetites of the time. O'Hara's fought for a full liquor license and, after much debate, was awarded with what was claimed to be the first full liquor license granted outside of downtown St. Cloud. O'Hara's became a hub for the town's St. Patrick's Day celebration, serving corned beef hash and green beer every year. During the 1980s, O'Hara's also emerged as one of St. Cloud's first sports bars. O'Hara's sponsored many local amateur Central Minnesota baseball, hockey and basketball teams. A large projection screen was added to the restaurant to air live games. The establishment was just outside of the television blackout radius for Minnesota Vikings football and Minnesota North Stars hockey, which meant that O'Hara's was allowed to show games that other St. Cloud bars were barred from airing. Some major sporting events were also pirated, including popular 1980s boxing matches, by a cable stream that was run into the restaurant from a nearby house.

By the mid-1990s, O'Hara's was ready to evolve and bring the next trend in beer to St. Cloud. At the time, Tim had already taken sole possession of the establishment. In addition to researching the Colorado breweries that Gallus had mentioned in his thank-you note, Tim traveled to visit breweries in Oregon, Arizona and Massachusetts for inspiration. He ended up purchasing tanks from Oregon and hiring a brewer, but the future star of the brewery's operation, Chris Laumb, arrived unsolicited, looking to fulfill a longtime dream.

Long before he tasted his first beer, Laumb seemed destined to one day be a part of the brewing industry. From a young age, he had been naturally interested in both history and science. Laumb grew up in St. Cloud, across the street from Riverside Park. He often ventured over to the park to go fishing in the Beaver Islands and to take part in his other favorite hobby: collecting old beer cans. Laumb dove through dumpsters in the park to find different designs from New Ulm's Schell's Brewery, products from the Cold Spring Brewing Company and many other beer products from both near and far. "Back in the '70s and '80s, there were a lot of odd-looking cans," Laumb said. "I was really interested in where all these places where." Laumb's mother also frequently began taking him on tours of the breweries that continued to operate throughout Minnesota. "I started smelling the smells and seeing all of the activities," Laumb said. "A lot of the buildings then were old, and all of the activity really planted a seed."

Laumb began performing in local bands when he turned eighteen; he claims it was initially to pick up girls. At this time, he began discovering beers that weren't the typical Budweiser, Miller and Coors varieties that dominated the Central Minnesota tap space. The same Schell's brewery that had a can design that Laumb had long been fond of released a pils and weisen that were unlike anything else in the market. Laumb also discovered imports like Guinness and Fosters. "It was amazing that beers could be so flavorful," Laumb said. "I always thought there had to be something better than what was being sold in the liquor stores."

When he was around twenty years old, Laumb discovered how people could brew at home. The science of the process and the ability to create unique and flavorful beers was intriguing to Laumb. At the time, however, there was a very limited selection of homebrewing supplies. The only kits available featured extract cans and packets of yeast. Laumb remembered that his first two batches turned out terribly, but he was hooked on the process of homebrewing and was determined to improve his craft. Already an avid reader, Laumb began searching for any book related to beer—everything from the scientific process of brewing to the storied history of humans making alcohol. Laumb then discovered Charlie Papazian's opus, *The Complete Joy of Homebrewing*. The Boulder, Colorado schoolteacher had been teaching a homebrewing class for years in his home, long before it was formally legalized by President Jimmy Carter in 1978. Papazian had been taught how to homebrew by a neighbor who had been doing so since the days of Prohibition. Papazian, too, searched high and low for any book about brewing, as his hobby morphed into an obsession. Disappointed by the selection of brewing books available and the emphasis they had on making beer cheaply rather than focusing on making quality beer, Papazian began writing a book that drastically changed American brewing. *The Complete Joy of Homebrewing* has sold several hundred thousand copies; it simplified the brewing process for its American audience and shared a variety of new recipes that were drastically different from the light lagers that dominated the market. The book was a spark of inspiration for a whole generation of craft brewers like Laumb, who started the more sophisticated process of all-grain homebrewing soon after reading it. "It was pretty mind blowing," Laumb said. "The book was so far ahead of its time."

For Laumb, homebrewing was initially just a hobby. He kept himself busy with music gigs and a full-time job with a local printing company. But one day, he read about O'Hara's plans to add the brewery to its facility in the *St. Cloud Times* newspaper. Laumb had only been to the storied bar and restaurant a handful of times and had no professional brewing experience, but something compelled him to ask the owners of the operation if they needed a brewer. Laumb also said that he had been discouraged when the printing company he worked for was sold to a Twin Cities–based company. One day, he built up his courage and drove over to O'Hara's to speak with Tim O'Hara. "I showed him pictures of our homebrew setup and practically begged him for a job," Laumb recalled.

O'Hara's had already hired a head brewer, but O'Hara hired Laumb as an apprentice under him. O'Hara's officially opened its brewery in 1996, operating on a ten-barrel system that had been built in Oregon. Before, the rest of the taps in St. Cloud and Central Minnesota had been overwhelmingly dominated by light lagers, as many of them catered to the college crowd. But after O'Hara's opened its brewery, freshly made ales were introduced to the market. "Initially, it was a tepid reaction," Laumb said. "O'Hara's was really far ahead of the curve. Maybe too far." After six months, the original head brewer left and Laumb took over the operation. "It felt like winning the lottery," Laumb said. He rotated the seasonal brews frequently and especially sought European inspiration for new brews. His honey wheat ale eventually became a best-seller. O'Hara's also brewed a stout, pale ale and red ale along with its seasonal brews. "I got a handle for designing beers and figured out what does work and what doesn't work," Laumb said. "I got really lucky to be able to do that."

Despite plenty of skepticism from Central Minnesota's core audience, who were conditioned to consuming light lagers, a cult following emerged for O'Hara's beers. Many future craft brewers who attended college in the Central Minnesota area later complimented Laumb for crafting their first preferences of craft beers. Other entrepreneurs and homebrewers throughout Minnesota came to O'Hara's to pick Laumb's brain about starting their own operations. Laumb was also an early member of the Minnesota Craft Brewers Guild, which was formed in 2000 with about a dozen industry members at the table. Now the group represents hundreds of breweries from across the state. The guild was initially formed to push a single issue: allow breweries to fill growlers to sell on site. The statute that had banned this practice since Prohibition was initially altered to allow brewpubs to sell off site in 2003; serving pints at breweries was later legalized with the Surly Bill in 2011. Sunday growler sales became legal in 2015, thanks to the efforts of the Minnesota Craft Brewers Guild lobby. Laumb also traveled to national beer conferences, where he once met his homebrew idol, Papazian. "I thanked him for showing me the light," Laumb said. "I'm sure he hears that every day."

When added competition arrived on the St. Cloud bar and restaurant scene in the mid-2000s, Tim O'Hara put a part of O'Hara's location on the market in 2006. However, he publicly pledged to keep the downstairs bar and brewery running. Later, in 2007, O'Hara's was given permission from the city council to remodel its interior and to create a space to rent out to a new tenant so that the brewery could continue operating. It appeared that a fresh look was coming to the more than sixty-year-old business, but just a few weeks later, a "Thank You" sign on the door notified patrons that the business had closed after sixty-two years. The news even came as a surprise to the now-late O'Hara's regular and longtime Stearns History Museum historian Bob Lommel, who was quoted in the *St. Cloud Times* article about the surprising closure.

While the May 2007 closure halted the brewery temporarily, the brewing equipment, under Laumb's direction and in his restaurant space, returned under a new name only a few months later. Little Falls resident Nick McCann teamed with business partner and Sartell resident Wendel Clark to create McCann's Food & Brew. The duo invested $600,000 into remodeling the old O'Hara's space, according to a *St. Cloud Times* report. Laumb resumed brewing his recipes and continued to experiment with seasonal brews. Pool tables and games were brought in as an attraction to McCann's, which served a variety of traditional bar food; it became known for its novelty two-pound burger eating challenge that came served on a shovel. The brewpub, however, shut its doors, after just five years in business, when its lease expired in 2012.

Laumb went on to work for the Cold Spring Brewing Company—the same brewery where he had toured and collected cans as a child.

There, he experienced brewing on an entirely different scale, which gave him the skills he needed for a groundbreaking project down the road. The 3308 Third Street North space later became Spicy Crab N' Crawfish, Cosmo's and New York Gyro. While O'Hara's and McCann's old brewing equipment has collected plenty of dust over the years, it was also resurrected by both Lupine Brewing and Pantown Brewing—but more on those breweries later.

GRANITE CITY FOOD & BREW

About a mile away from where O'Hara's once stood, another brewpub was launched and proceeded to take St. Cloud's nickname across the country. Granite City Food & Brew opened in 1999 at 3945 Second Street South in St. Cloud, and it has grown to operate several locations in more than a dozen states. Its staff members all around the country are taught the brewpub chain's St. Cloud origins and how it was named after the Central Minnesota city's local moniker. The history lesson is also printed on all of Granite City's menus. The St. Cloud location celebrated its twentieth anniversary with a celebration in the summer of 2019.

Before the name Granite City was selected, the restaurant's co-founders, Steve Wagenheim and Bill Burdick, planned to revive the St. Cloud Brewing Company name, and they planned on naming a beer Old Heidelberger in honor of the shuttered brewery's history. The duo, who have since left the company, also initially made public plans to renovate the Lahr building on St. Germain Street in St. Cloud's downtown. They hoped to host an Oktoberfest celebration at the restaurant's opening that would cater to the widespread German heritage in Central Minnesota. The location and name ultimately fell through, but Wagenheim and Burdick continued to pursue the concept under the Granite City title. Granite quarries have operated in St. Cloud and the surrounding area for well over one hundred years. The steps and exterior base of the Minnesota state capitol building in St. Paul were even constructed with granite from Stearns County.

Wagenheim is a restaurant industry veteran. The Michigan State University graduate found success before Granite City when he operated a sports bar restaurant chain called Champps. The multi-state chain had evolved from a St. Paul restaurant called Concourse 7, which had opened in 1984. Wagenheim helped expand the company to more than fifty locations while he served as its president and CEO. Since leaving Granite City in 2013, Wagenheim has gone on to create Pub 42 Restaurant and Bar.

Burdick came into the project as an experienced brewer. He had brewed at Minnetonka's Sherlock's Home Restaurant Pub and Brewery for a decade by the time Granite City was launched in 1999 outside of downtown St. Cloud. Burdick brought cask ales and firkins to Minnesota craft beer drinkers at the brewpub Sherlock's Home, which operated from 1989 to 2002. Burdick was also a frequent author of books about beer chemistry, history and other topics for various publications. He innovated brewing at Granite City, and after the brewpub found success in St. Cloud, it expanded to a second location in Sioux Falls, South Dakota.

As the brewpub continued to rapidly expand, Burdick searched for a way to keep Granite City beers consistent from one town to the next, no matter how far away they were. Using his chemistry knowledge, Burdick developed a process patented as Fermentus Interruptus that the company continues to use. At Granite City, the sugar water used to make beer called wort is made at a central location. The wort is then refrigerated below thirty-six degrees Fahrenheit to stave off any yeast fermentation. The wort is then transported to each location, where the beer is fermented on site. Not only did the process improve consistency across the country, but it allows the company to operate with less equipment.

Sioux Falls was initially the central wort brewing location for the Granite City chain. The chain's headquarters eventually shifted, in 2005, to a small Iowa town off Interstate 25. Ellsworth, Iowa, is the kind of town that, if you blink, you just might miss it. Located about thirty miles north of Ames, Iowa, and the Iowa State University campus, the town has just over five hundred residents. Here, an unmarked brewery supplies wort for the entire chain. The location was built in this town because of its strategic positioning off of a major interstate road and its high-quality water. Each Granite City location still has its own brewer who oversees fermentation. St. Cloud still gets to brew some beers from scratch, and it serves as a pilot brewery for small-batch brews.

Many of the beers made at Granite City take inspiration from Central Minnesota. Granite City's all-time best seller is its German-style Bennie Bock, which was named after the nearby College of St. Benedict. The Bennie Bock even went on to win a silver medal at the 2018 Great American Beer Festival. Each Granite City location now displays a replica of the medal. Granite City has always had a core lineup of the Northern lager, Broad Axe stout and the Duke pale ale. A 76-IBU double IPA called Batch 1,000 and a

German-style wheat hefeweizen called Prairie Vixen have also been added to the brewpub chain's year-round offerings. A popular order at Granite City is a half-Bennie Bock with a half-Northern—a customer tradition that began in St. Cloud. Granite City also debuts a rotating seasonal beer every month. The brewpub has experimented with everything from hazy IPAs and Belgian strongs to an annual Oktoberfest Marzen lager. "What's exciting about being a brewer today is the endless experimentation," said R.J. Nab, Granite City's vice president brewmaster.

Food is also an essential part of Granite City's success. In St. Cloud, the brewpub is well known for its Sunday brunch buffet and large portions. The restaurant serves a diverse menu that includes something for everyone: bar food, sandwiches, burgers, salads, pasta, entrées and steaks. Each menu item also comes with a recommended beer pairing. The exact menus of each location vary by region, but Granite City employs a central executive chef. Beer is not just for drinking at Granite City; it's used as an ingredient in a variety of dishes to add subtle flavors.

The Granite City chain filed for Chapter 11 bankruptcy in December 2019; increased competition and the growth of home-delivery food services were referenced in the filing. A new owner, who also took over Cadillac Ranch restaurants, swooped in to purchase the chain. The parent company of the regional barbecue chain Famous Dave's agreed to purchase the Granite City chain for $3.65 million. Jeff Crivello, the CEO of the Minnetonka, Minnesota–based BBQ Holdings, said that the acquisition was intended for "our growth and expansion as a multi-brand restaurant company" in a press release about the transaction.

7

BEAVER ISLAND BREWING ARRIVES

Explorer Zebulon Pike, during his 1805 Mississippi River expedition through St. Cloud, once stumbled upon a number of beavers building dams on a group of islands. The explorer for whom Pikes Peak is known dubbed the islands the Beaver Islands, and they have since become some of St. Cloud's most recognizable and defining natural features. The Beaver Islands are a collection of fifteen or so islands—the number fluctuates depending on the Mississippi River's water level. The grouping sits just below the St. Cloud Dam and runs south, to the St. Cloud Country Club. The cascading islands are most often visible to those crossing the University Bridge near St. Cloud State University.

The Beaver Islands were used for camping, picnics and other purposes during the 1930s. The largest island once featured an athletic field that was used by St. Cloud State University. One of the most prominent islands, Sportsman Island, was also used as a public park for several years. Bridges even connected many of the islands at one time. Today, St. Cloud State University still owns the majority of the Beaver Islands, but they are of little use to the public. Trees and wildlife occupy the island grouping, which functions as a floodplain forest when the Mississippi River rises every spring. The legacy of the Beaver Islands, however, lives on, thanks to the town's most successful craft brewery.

Beaver Island Brewing Co. was launched in early 2015 and introduced St. Cloud to the emerging craft beer taproom culture. The operation has since put St. Cloud back on the map for brewing by collecting both Great

Barrel-aged beers at Beaver Island Brewing Co.'s taproom in St. Cloud. *Courtesy of Andrew Webster.*

A flight at the Beaver Island Brewing Co. taproom. *Courtesy of Andrew Webster.*

Tanks at the original Beaver Island Brewing Co. brewery in St. Cloud. *Courtesy of Andrew Webster.*

American Beer Festival and World Beer Cup medals. It's also fitting that the brewery has garnered a special cult following for its chocolate oatmeal stout called Sweet Mississippi, which was named after the river that flows through the Beaver Islands and the heart of St. Cloud.

After operating for just three years, Beaver Island Brewing was recognized as one of the country's fastest-growing craft breweries by the Brewers Association, a national trade group. It is one of the few craft beer operations that was launched during Minnesota's 2010s brewery boom that has gone on to become more than just a taproom. Beaver Island Brewing is a full-production brewery, with its own canning and bottling facility. The brewery's production spot is located in a separate location from its taproom and was constructed several years before its trio of co-founders ever dreamed of or predicted its existence in their original business plan.

Every year, the brewery hosts Oktoberfest and Maibockfest events with the City of St. Cloud, where many attendees come dressed in traditional German garb, including lederhosen and dirndls. Beaver Island Brewing has also hosted public canoe outings, where the brewery has led Mississippi

River expeditions through the islands that inspired their name. "Never in my wildest dreams did I ever think we could grow so quickly," said Nick Barth, one of Beaver Island's three co-founders. "Our recipe for success is a great team that has a bunch of different complementing strengths."

A decade before Beaver Island Brewing was launched, Barth had a different fermented drink of choice. The St. Cloud Apollo High School graduate had originally returned home in 2005, after attending college in Alaska and living briefly in Colorado, to start a wine bar. Barth's family had previously launched an intimate theater and concert venue on Fifth Street, in the heart of the downtown of St. Cloud, called Pioneer Place, and they recruited Nick home to launch a bar called the Veranda Lounge. The bar was meant to occupy guests before, during and after the intermissions of the Pioneer Place's performances, with a wide wine selection and martinis. "St. Cloud was in a revitalization phase at the time," Barth said.

When Barth first arrived back in his hometown, he was newly twenty-one years old, and his diet largely consisted of two-for-one burgers and twenty-five-cent tacos. But his palate soon became much more sophisticated when he became a certified sommelier—a wine expert who must pass a blind taste test to earn certification. He also later opened a downtown St. Cloud liquor store specializing in wine. Ironically, as a sommelier, Barth was called to testify in front of Minnesota's legislature for the 2011 Surly Bill—the very piece of legislation that later allowed Beaver Island Brewing to open a public taproom. While most of the bill's laws pertained to the deregulation of the brewing industry, his sommelier expertise was used to argue for a smaller portion of the bill that impacted the wine industry. "I had no idea at the time that I would be opening a brewery a few years later," Barth said. "We would have never been able to open Beaver Island without [the Surly Bill]."

Barth's affinity for craft beer was slowly developed after he became a wine expert. He remembered trying the beers at Granite City Food & Brewery and said he always ordered the house brews when he dined there. The Veranda Lounge soon began stocking beers from craft beer pioneers, like Oregon's Deschutes Brewery and Colorado's New Belgium Brewing, when it began expanding its distribution footprints eastward. The Barths also purchased and began operating a storied downtown St. Cloud college bar called D.B. Searle's. While the location—considered to be one of St. Cloud's most haunted spots—was long known for its "nickel night" light beer promotions, the Barths added craft brews to the bar's tap lines. D.B. Searle's began featuring a number of Third Street Brewhouse's products when the Cold Spring brewery expanded its rebranded craft beer line. Barth also opened a trendy farm-to-table restaurant on the third floor, above D.B. Searle's, which offered a handful of craft beers. "I was just like the consumer today," Barth said. "I was really interested in what was new. I wanted to try what was different."

While his thirst for craft beer was growing, Barth became acquainted with another St. Cloud native through the Veranda Lounge: Matt Studer. Studer had graduated from St. Cloud Tech High School in 2000 and remained in town to attend St. Cloud Technical and Community College for an education in sales and management. He had grown up as a family friend of the O'Hara family, who introduced him to craft beer at their brewpub. Shortly after graduating from high school, Studer's eventual wife, Vicki, gifted him with a Mr. Beer brewing kit. The one-gallon starter brewing system has remained one of the most popular at-home brewing kits for more than two decades. Many brewers have gotten their start on the remarkably simple system, which uses a plastic fermenter and stovetop instructions. The beer he made wasn't particularly good, but Studer was intrigued by the whole process and began understanding the science that went into brewing. "It didn't turn out at all, but, of course, you drank it because you wanted it to," Studer said.

After two Mr. Beer–kit batches, Studer looked into upgrading his system, and he soon got the idea to use O'Hara's growlers instead of individual bottles to more efficiently package his homebrews. Studer also doubled the amount of sugar that he had previously used in the bottles for carbonation—which ended up over-carbonating and blowing shards of his growlers all over the basement of his friend's new house that he was living in at the time. Studer eventually learned from that lesson and perfected his homebrewing recipes. He soon built his own all-grain brewing system and started dreaming of opening his own brewery. "I think every homebrewer thinks about that in the back of their mind," Studer said. "And, of course, family and friends are so nice and say your beers are so good and that you should do it commercially."

At the time, Studer was a realtor by profession and started toying with the idea of opening a brewery with his friends. Some of his real estate clients also had the idea to open a brewery, as breweries began to line the streets of Minnesota's cities after the passage of the 2011 Surly Bill. Studer even showed St. Cloud building locations to Aaron Rieland, who eventually launched St. Joseph's Bad Habit Brewing. After a showing, Studer told him of his plans to open his own brewery, and the two met for an exploratory lunch to discuss their visions; ultimately, they had different ideas, wished each other luck and went their separate ways. Studer also showed former O'Hara's and McCann's brewer Chris Laumb some locations for a potential

St. Cloud brewery. Again, Studer shared his own intentions, and Laumb was sufficiently intrigued. The two stayed in touch. Laumb and Studer had mutual acquaintances in the St. Cloud music industry, and Studer had previously shared some of his homebrews with Laumb, looking for feedback. "He said it was good, but I'm not sure if he actually liked it or was just being nice," Studer joked. "Deep down, I always thought he would be the perfect brewmaster for the brewery I wanted."

As Studer's plans for a brewery became more serious, he also formed a closer bond with Barth. Eventually, Studer invited Barth over for one of his homebrew sessions, and the sessions became a weekly Tuesday tradition between the two. Because of his newfound affinity for craft beer, Barth set a 2013 New Year's resolution to sell a batch of beer that he brewed himself. He accomplished this when he sold a six-pack of his homebrew to his father. The entrepreneur inside Barth also started to notice the boom of craft beer in Minnesota after the Surly Bill—the same piece of legislation that he had testified for—was signed into law.

During their weekly homebrew sessions, Barth and Studer began making a serious business plan for their own craft brewery. They began conducting research by visiting numerous Twin Cities craft breweries. They were particularly blown away by Minneapolis's Dangerous Man Brewing Co. Studer and his wife, when they went to visit family near Portland, Oregon, made excursions to breweries of all types and sizes. Barth and Studer also visited the 2014 Craft Brewers Conference in Denver, Colorado, where they attended seminars and picked the brains of brewers from across the country. During their trip to Denver, Barth and Studer also toured a number of established Colorado craft breweries. "Everyone was so open and willing to share things with us," Barth said. "We learned how different the brewing industry was—in that it is very open and collaborative."

While Studer and Barth had only been homebrewing, they realized that brewing commercially was a whole different ballgame. They soon spoke with Laumb, who was still working the nightshift at Third Street Brewhouse and had the experience they were looking for. Laumb was very intrigued by their ideas and strongly believed that his hometown deserved its own craft brewery taproom. He signed on to be the operation's head brewmaster. "They are really good at the business side, which I am not," Laumb said. "I am a process, creative guy, and they are businessmen. It's a team where we all had our strengths to bring to the table."

Like the founders of Granite City Food & Brew before them, the trio behind Beaver Island Brewing Co. initially planned to resurrect the St.

Cloud Brewing Company name. They built a business plan behind the title, even registering the www.STCBREW.com web domain name, and had the old brewery logo recommissioned. The trio later got cold feet about committing to the name, thinking that it would limit the operation if it ever expanded beyond a regional brewery. Pantown Brewing, named after a St. Cloud neighborhood, was later considered, but it was already registered by St. Cloud realtor Noel Johnson—who eventually opened his own St. Cloud brewery under the name in late 2018. Instead, the trio finally chose the iconic Mississippi River Beaver Islands as their inspiration for the brewery's name, as it was a way to honor St. Cloud without sacrificing future marketing capabilities.

After settling on a name, the trio needed to find a location for Beaver Island Brewing Co. Initially, the trio was set on a space in the heart of downtown St. Cloud, next to the Barths' D.B. Searle's. But the location was occupied by a Jimmy John's fast-food restaurant that didn't want to give up its prime real estate. So the trio found the brewery's eventual downtown St. Cloud location at a Sixth Avenue strip mall that had been built in 1939 and had two connected spaces available.

One of the spaces had previously belonged to a popular Central Minnesota sandwich chain called Bo Diddley's Pub & Deli. The regional favorite was opened in 1981 in St. Joseph and expanded with multiple St. Cloud locations. The eatery served subs, pita pockets, gyros and shawarma, and it was frequently voted as the town's favorite sandwich shop during numerous "best of" polls. While the restaurant shared the name of a rock 'n' roll pioneer, its founder, John Forsythe, long swore that the nickname was his own from his time at St. John's University—he was nicknamed "Bo" by his friends, who then added on other monikers like "Diddley," as in "diddling around." Forsythe once told the *St. Cloud Times*: "In the little farm town where I'm from, we weren't listening to Bo Diddley. We were listening to Hank Williams." Still, the restaurant faced numerous copyright battles with the late musician and his estate after he died of heart failure in 2008. The restaurant chain was consolidating its operations and opening another St. Cloud location when it, somewhat surprisingly, closed its downtown spot in the spring of 2014. The other portion of the building had previously belonged to Pickard Motors. The Chrysler car dealership and auto shop had been run by the father-son duo of Frank Pickard Sr. and Frank Pickard Jr. for a number of decades.

Beaver Island Brewing configured the building to comprise just under five thousand square feet—saving it from the expensive city code requirements that were imposed on larger buildings. A 1950s Graco lube table with "lubrication station" engraved into it was left by Pickard Motors and was repurposed for the brewery's iconic tap station. Similarly, old bowling alley lanes from St. Cloud's former Granite Bowl South were repurposed for the taproom's bar top. The Beaver Island Brewing's taproom is also decorated with St. Cloud–made bricks, cattle barn lights from the Minnesota State Fair and other repurposed items from Central Minnesota farms. The brewery's brand-new stainless-steel brewing tanks were made by a fellow St. Cloud company called DCI. They were delivered to Beaver Island Brewing on December 12, 2014, and were assembled almost immediately. "We unwrapped them like a kid on Christmas morning," Barth told the *St. Cloud Times* when the tanks arrived. "It's like when you were a kid and got to open a Christmas present on December 23."

The brewery's trio of founders mostly built the brewery and taproom by themselves—outside of the skilled plumbing and electrical work. They spent countless hours and evenings inside the facility. "It was a lot of work," Laumb said. "But it was really cool to see the fruits of your labor come together." After months of hype and people prodding the Beaver Island Brewing founders for an opening date, the public got its first taste of the brewery's beer at the January 24, 2015 St. Cloud Craft Beer Festival. The annual event is organized by local radio station company Leighton Broadcasting and is held in downtown St. Cloud, at the River's Edge Convention Center. It had debuted four years prior to Beaver Island's arrival and had quickly become a popular, sold-out event, where thousands of attendees got unlimited pours of beers from around the country. The local bars that surround the event host numerous tap takeover events. Hundreds of people make the trek up from the Twin Cities to attend; it's become St. Cloud's largest annual celebration of beer.

Beaver Island Brewing had a steadily long line at its first event, as many patrons were looking to get a taste of the new brewery. Beaver Island Brewing debuted with four beers to sample: a German-style kolsch called Ripple that was designed to convert light beer drinkers; a red IPA named '39, after the year that St. Cloud Brewing Company closed and the year that the building that housed Beaver Island Brewing's taproom had been built; a winter ale porter with 9.1 percent alcohol called Union Suit that was named after the onesie pajama of the same name; and a double IPA called Lane 5 that had five hop varieties and was named after the bowling alley lanes that were repurposed for the brewery's taproom bar top. Beaver Island Brewing claimed the event's people's choice award at their debut. Beaver Island Brewing has since been a fixture at the event and has claimed several other awards.

Beaver Island then hit the market with a three-day, ten-stop Central Minnesota bar tour in early February 2015. The taproom opened later that same month and, in true craft beer fashion, has hosted food trucks ever since. While the brewery's consumers still required plenty of education on craft beers, Laumb said that the public had a much better understanding of craft beer during this debut than O'Hara's, which he had experienced two decades earlier. A number of other St. Cloud bars began clamoring for Beaver Island beers; today, a majority of places with beer taps in Central Minnesota carry their products. The Beaver Island Brewing taproom initially had a chalkboard with a list of places that carried its beer, but it was quickly removed because the list became too long to maintain.

While Beaver Island Brewing was a success right out of the gate, neither Barth, Studer nor Laumb cashed a paycheck during its inaugural year. Studer maintained his real estate position, and many of his final deals were inked at the tables of the Beaver Island Brewing taproom. He and Barth initially helped bartend in the taproom, and Studer also helped Laumb brew and keg beers—often working long hours late into the evening. The brewery initially made all of its account deliveries itself. And while the trio of founders were putting in long hours, they sensed that their new brewery was about to blossom beyond their original vision. "The beer culture of St. Cloud and Central Minnesota has absolutely shifted," Barth said. "There's an awareness for craft beer, with people enjoying more profound and unique flavors."

8

THE REEMERGENCE OF ST. CLOUD BEER

More than one hundred years after the Old Heidelberger beer got its name from a public naming contest in St. Cloud, Beaver Island Brewing unknowingly branded its eventual signature beer in the same fashion. Sticky notes were scattered throughout the Beaver Island taproom in May 2015, and patrons were asked to submit names for the brewery's upcoming chocolate oatmeal stout release. Samples of the beer were made available to patrons for inspiration. Beaver Island Brewing's head brewer, Chris Laumb, modeled the brew after a popular stout called Buffalo Sweat made by Tallgrass Brewing of Manhattan, Kansas. Laumb had contract brewed that beer during his tenure at Third Street Brewhouse. Laumb put his own twist on this style, using British malts and organic Ecuadorian cocoa nibs.

The winning entry of the naming contest was actually submitted as "Mississippi Sweet," but Beaver Island Brewing swapped the order of the words; thus, the Sweet Mississippi stout was named. "[Most] importantly, nobody had used it yet," Beaver Island co-founder Nick Barth told the *St. Cloud Times* when the winning entry was announced. Sweet Mississippi was formally released in July 2015 as a seasonal brew. The variety returned the next spring to much fanfare, but again, it was just a seasonal brew. Eventually, the demand for Sweet Mississippi forced it to become a year-round flagship beer. It's now the most heavily produced Beaver Island Brewing beer, and it claimed a bronze medal at the 2018 U.S. Open Beer Championship. "I knew it would be successful but had no idea it would be as successful as it is," Laumb said. "As a stout, it remains strong in the summer months, which is crazy to me.…It's also a great base beer to [do] wacky stuff, like adding coconut and coffee. You can really play around with it."

Laumb has also claimed prestigious awards for other Beaver Island Brewing beers. The brewery's first major medal came when its Oktoberfest brew won bronze at the 2017 Great American Beer Festival. The annual Denver beer festival and competition was co-founded by homebrew icon Charlie Papazian in 1982, and it is currently considered the "Super Bowl" of the commercial brewing industry. At the competition, judges typically award a gold, silver and bronze medal in about one hundred unique categories. Several thousand breweries from across the country enter the competition each year. No one from Beaver Island Brewing was present to accept the brewery's medal and receive an honorary fist bump and photo from Papazian in 2017, but the founders quickly learned of their victory. Laumb remembered that he was sitting on his couch when the awards were announced; he had found an online livestream of the awards ceremony and had turned it on just in the nick of time—the Oktoberfest category was announced just minutes after he started watching. "It was super cool and something I never thought would happen,"

Sweet Mississippi stout at Beaver Island Brewing Co. *Courtesy of Andrew Webster.*

Laumb said. "Being recognized like that gives you some [credibility] and certainly helps push some product." Meanwhile, Barth had just finished a long bicycle ride and was going to take a shower when his phone started blowing up with congratulatory texts and Twitter messages. The Great American Beer Festival medal has helped Beaver Island Brewing's Oktoberfest become even more popular than it was before. The German-style beer is released every fall, and the brewery hosts a city celebration in its honor.

The Beaver Island Brewing Oktoberfest celebration is typically held annually in September. But the brewery wasn't early to this party; the official Oktoberfest is held in Munich, Germany, every September. The original Oktoberfest was held in 1810, in honor of the Bavarian crown prince Ludwig's marriage to Princess Therese von Sachsen-Hildburghausen. The festivities began on October 12, 1810, and ended on October 17 with a horse race. In the following years, the celebrations were repeated, and later, the festival was prolonged and moved forward, into September, as it allowed for better weather conditions—something Minnesotans can certainly understand. Like the official Munich celebration, Beaver Island Brewing's Oktoberfest officially starts when St. Cloud's mayor taps the first keg.

Beaver Island Brewing also has a pair of bronze medals on display in its taproom for its Check Pils beer. The cleverly named, hockey-themed Czech pilsner was originally brewed in 2018, when St. Cloud hosted the 2018 Hockey Day Minnesota, organized by regional sports television station Fox Sports North. Like many cities in Minnesota, St. Cloud has a long hockey history. St. Cloud Cathedral High School graduate Nate Schmidt went on to have a career in the NHL, and St. Cloud State University has both Division I men's and women's hockey programs. The men's team was brought to Division I by former "Miracle on Ice" Olympic coach Herb Brooks and has become a consistent powerhouse; the team made the NCAA Frozen Four in the 2012 and 2013 seasons and has produced numerous NHL players. Check Pils first won a bronze medal at the 2018 U.S. Beer Open—the same event where Sweet Mississippi had previously won a medal. Later in 2018, Check Pils won another bronze medal at the 2018 World Beer Cup. The event is held every other year at the Craft Brewers Conference, and in 2018, more than eight thousand beers from sixty-six countries competed in the contest. It was the first time that Beaver Island Brewing had ever entered the World Beer Cup competition.

Beaver Island Brewing has also experimented well beyond traditional beer styles. One of the brewery's first limited releases was a Belgian single called One Speed. The beer was made with all-organic ingredients, including imported Belgian yeast and malts and German hops. The brewery also takes a colonial approach to its annual seasonal called Tip-Up. The beer is brewed with spruce tips, which impact both the beer's taste and aroma; the ingredient was said to have been popular in early American beer as a replacement for hops, which weren't readily available at the time. Legend has it that Benjamin Franklin previously brewed beer with spruce tips.

The most unique of Beaver Island Brewing's beers, however, is also its most Minnesotan. The brewery released the first lefse beer to ever be commercially released. Minnesota has a strong Scandinavian heritage, and the Norwegian potato bread called lefse is commonly baked in the North Star State, especially around the holidays. The beer called Uffda Ale was made exclusively for the Minnesota State Fair, an annual event that starts at the end of August and runs through Labor Day and is affectionately known as the "Great Minnesota Get-Together." The Minnesota State Fair is considered to be the second-largest state fair in the United States; with around two million attendees, it only trails the Texas State Fair. The Minnesota State Fair has long been known for its food offerings, with hundreds of vendors in attendance that specialize in foods that are put on a stick and deep fried and overflowing buckets of freshly baked cookies. After the Surly Bill was passed and numerous Minnesota breweries were launched, a beer garden featuring all of Minnesota's local brews emerged as a popular attraction at the fair, and Beaver Island Brewing looked to make a splash with its lefse beer.

After coming up with the idea for the lefse beer, Laumb researched to see if any lefse beers had previously been released. While there were some named lefse, Laumb couldn't find any that were actually brewed with the bread. "I figured, 'This is a starch, there is no reason we can't brew with this,'" Laumb said. "But I also had no idea how it would react. 'Would it dissolve or stay in the mash?'" After a couple pilot batches, Laumb found that the lefse dissolved as he desired. For the Uffda Ale, Beaver Island Brewing sourced its lefse from Norsland Lefse in Rushton—a town in southeastern Minnesota with a population of fewer than two thousand people. Norsland Lefse is run by one of Laumb's distant cousins. Uffda Ale also used a Norwegian fruit called lingonberries as added sweetness. Laumb humorously described the brew as a "Lutheran church dinner in a glass." The beer, which was garnished with an actual slice of lefse, was an overwhelming hit at the Minnesota State Fair. A popular Minneapolis media company called City Pages ranked Uffda Ale among the best of the twenty-five specialty craft beers that were featured at the 2018 Minnesota State Fair. Twin Cities–based television station Kare 11 also featured the beer during its fair programming.

In the past, Beaver Island Brewing has also looked to music for inspiration for its brews. The brewery once released a beer called Crosby Pilsen Mash, which was named after the supergroup Crosby, Stills and Nash. The beer also paid homage to Crosby Hop Farm in Woodburn, Oregon—a regular supplier of Beaver Island Brewing. Mash is a brewing term for mixing crushed malts with hot water. Beaver Island Brewing also created a beer named after a popular St. Cloud–based classic rock cover band called the Fabulous Armadillos. Annually, the group has the highest-attended Summertime by George concert and puts on themed cover shows throughout the state. The sessions IPA, originally called Fabulous Armadillo, has since been renamed Tribute as a way to expand its distribution without licensing concerns.

During the first year of its existence, Beaver Island Brewing delivered all of its beer itself. And once it hit most of the accounts available in Central Minnesota, it expanded north, to Duluth. Because the brewery was self-distributing, Barth had to make weekly trips to Duluth by himself; the round-trip trek is more than four hours. His long trips ended, however, in January 2016, when Beaver Island Brewing began distributing its beer through St. Cloud–based Bernick's. The Pepsi distributor also handles a number of craft beer brands. Barth credited Bernick's partnership and distribution reach as the main reason that Beaver Island Brewing was named the fortieth-fastest-growing small and independent brewery in the country in 2018 by the Brewers Association, an industry trade group. Beaver Island Brewing also added a new production facility to the business in spring 2017, which allowed the brewery to offer six-packs in liquor stores. The site at 401 Electron Drive in the St. Cloud Airport Business Park now handles canning and the majority of Beaver Island Brewing's beer production. The brewery's original taproom still serves as its pilot bar for small-batch beers. Beaver Island Brewing started distributing to the Twin Cities in February 2018 and is looking to continue measured growth in the future.

LUPINE BREWING CO.

Just over a month before the public got its first taste of Beaver Island Brewing, another brewery got its start in St. Cloud with some familiar equipment. Lupine Brewing Co. was launched in December 2014 in the old O'Hara's Brewpub and Restaurant and McCann's Food & Brew location at 3320

Third Street North in St. Cloud. Lupine never intended to stay in St. Cloud, and the operation, which has since moved to Delano, was just looking to get a head start on its production and distribution with turnkey equipment. But in this process, Lupine officially became St. Cloud's first distributing craft brewery since the St. Cloud Brewing Company closed in 1939, and it built a brief cult following among St. Cloud's patrons.

Lupine Brewing was named after the Latin phrase that means "resembling the wolf." The brewery was a midlife project for three Hanover friends: James Anderle, his childhood next-door neighbor Eric Sargent and his then-current neighbor Mike Dumas. They all had previous careers; Anderle worked in the healthcare industry, Sargent was a robotics engineer and Dumas was an internet salesman. The trio homebrewed together and had long talked about starting a business. Their research continually circled them back to joining the emerging craft beer industry.

The founders had long known that they wanted to build a taproom in the western Twin Cities suburbs near their Hanover residences. But when real estate deals kept falling through, they decided to take advantage of the old O'Hara's Brewpub and Restaurant and McCann's Food & Brew equipment that had just been collecting dust. This location gave them an opportunity to build their brand and get their beers on the market. The old brewpub space had been stripped down to a shell of itself when they took over. Lupine had no intention of fixing up the space to invite the public in; it, instead, wanted the building's production capabilities.

The trio of founders started brewing an IPA and a brown stout in November 2014, and they hit the market at St. Cloud–area bar accounts the following month. In January 2015, the trio was looking to hire a head brewer with previous experience and found one in Grant Aldrich. The brewer, whose height was imposing, was the brother of former NBA star and Minnesota native Cole Aldrich. The six-foot-eleven Cole had been a collegiate basketball star at University of Kansas, winning a national title in 2008, and was later drafted into the NBA in 2010 as the eleventh overall pick. He eventually started a journeyman career that included playing for the Oklahoma City Thunder, Houston Rockets, Sacramento Kings, New York Knicks, Los Angeles Clippers and his hometown Minnesota Timberwolves before he took his hoops career overseas. Grant, meanwhile, found his passion in beer. The Bloomington, Minnesota native started homebrewing extract kits with a former co-worker, which eventually led him to making a honey wine called mead. Grant got his first professional brewing job with Marshall-based Brau Brothers Brewing Co. in 2012. When he was hired, Brau's brewery was located in Lucan, which has a population of fewer than two hundred people. There, he helped the operation move to its Marshall facility.

Grant was intrigued when he noticed that Lupine had an opening for a head brewer. He showed up for his job interview with ten different homebrew creations for the trio of founders to sample. "With every single one, there was something good and unique about them," Anderle told the *St. Cloud Times*. "We were really impressed. We learned he had talent and creativity." Shortly after hiring Grant, Lupine gained serious credibility in the Minnesota brewing scene. The brewery that was relatively unknown at the time won the Lord Dabbler's Cup at the Beer Dabbler Winter Carnival for its cranberry oatmeal stout. The recipe was based on a homebrew created by the brewery's three founders and was voted the best beer by the attendees of the sold-out event; 7,500 people and around 120 breweries attended the festivities at the Minnesota State Fairgrounds. Immediately after the event, Lupine Brewing was in high demand to be put on tap across Central Minnesota and the Twin Cities.

Grant helped expand Lupine's portfolio with exotic brews. He once brewed a tea-infused American amber called Convocation and a cayenne pepper stout that was equal parts spicy and sweet. Lupine eventually got a license to fill growlers in St. Cloud and did so weekly in a corner of the building; this drew regular crowds.

Lupine eventually found a 3,500-square-foot space that overlooked the Crow River Valley and had been built in the early 1900s in Delano. They gutted the interior, replaced exterior bricks, updated the windows and restored the original floors and tin ceiling. They upgraded to a twenty-barrel brewhouse and three-barrel pilot system, and they used repurposed wood to build a crescent-shaped bar. The operation slowly ceased its operations in St. Cloud and opened its Delano taproom on August 8, 2015. But the operation still cherishes its beginnings and the following it built in St. Cloud.

Pantown Brewing Co.

After Lupine Brewing moved out, the old O'Hara's Brewpub and Restaurant and McCann's Food & Brew equipment again sat dormant. The building and equipment's owner, Noel Johnson, advertised the turnkey operation's availability but was ultimately unable to get any serious offers. The successful realtor and youth hockey coach, however, kept running the idea of starting his own brewery in the back of his mind.

Johnson had the foresight to register the Pantown Brewing Co. name in 2013 without any firm plans; he couldn't let anyone else get the name that related to one of St. Cloud's most infamous characters and periods of history. Pantown, a region where nearly sixty homes were built in 1917 to support the labor force of the short-lived and controversial Pan Motor Car Co., is still recognized as a neighborhood of St. Cloud. The car company was the vision of Mississippi-born insurance salesman Sam Pandolfo, who wanted St. Cloud to rival Detroit as the automaking hub of the United States. He found investors in St. Cloud and was intrigued by the area's proximity to the railroad and its natural resources; he was also interested in the area's availability of hardworking German laborers. Pandolfo wanted to make Pantown its own city inside of a city and had designed plans for a volunteer fire department, police department and school.

The Pan Motor Co. produced about 750 pan cars in five years—many are collectors' items today. The vehicles had extra compartments in the rear to hold tools, extra gas, oil, water and ice, and the front seats reclined to

Pantown Brewing in St. Cloud shortly after it opened in late 2018. *Courtesy of Andrew Webster.*

Brewing tanks are visible to customers at Pantown Brewing in St. Cloud. *Courtesy of Andrew Webster.*

The bar top at Pantown Brewing in St. Cloud. *Courtesy of Andrew Webster.*

A beer at Pantown Brewing in St. Cloud. *Courtesy of Andrew Webster.*

The taproom at Pantown Brewing in St. Cloud. *Courtesy of Andrew Webster.*

make beds. But Pandolfo's dream crumbled shortly after it was realized, when he was convicted of fraud relating to the sale of Pan Motor Co. stock. Future Major League Baseball commissioner Judge Kenesaw Mountain Landis oversaw Pandolfo's jury trial. Pandolfo ultimately served over two years at Leavenworth Federal Penitentiary. Historians still debate whether he was an elaborate con man or just an overzealous entrepreneur. He later died in Alaska after attempting other ventures in the production of washing machines, folded metal chairs, potato mashers and greaseless doughnuts. Pantown Park, a St. Cloud street, is still named after him.

Pantown Brewing Co. was eventually opened in December 2018 in the heart of the Pantown neighborhood in an old coffee roasting plant at 408 Thirty-Seventh Avenue North. Johnson partnered with Marty Czech to launch the brand; Czech had long been a key figure in St. Cloud's rugby community, coaching the St. Cloud State University team and the town's co-op high school squad called the Steelheads. Czech grew up in the shadows of a beer hub in Milwaukee, Wisconsin, and he moved to St. Cloud in 1996 to attend St. Cloud State University. Czech's parents purchased a homebrewing kit for him for his twentieth birthday, and he developed a palate for craft beer after he turned twenty-one and became a patron of O'Hara's Brewpub, where his sister worked as a server. Czech especially fell in love with O'Hara's raspberry wheat beer. "Twenty years ago, drinking out of my mug club glass, I couldn't imagine I would own the equipment and be brewing on it," Czech said. "I am so honored I get to carry on the tradition of the brewery that made me fall in love with beer."

Czech eventually became a realtor and was introduced to Johnson during a mutual transaction in 2012. After the deal was completed, Czech joined Johnson's firm. They eventually shared their mutual admiration for beer, and Johnson began recruiting Czech to be a partner in his brewery. Czech initially turned the opportunity down because of his rugby commitments. Czech said, "I thought about it for a week, and figured, 'How many opportunities do you come across to start a brewery?'"

The duo initially looked to open Pantown Brewing in the old O'Hara's Brewpub and Restaurant and McCann's Food & Brew space, but they ultimately decided that they needed a new location. Pantown Brewing, instead, revamped another Johnson-owned, 4,200-square-foot building in the heart of Pantown that was previously used as a coffee roasting plant called Muggsy's Beans. The duo debated whether the location would be a brewpub but came to the consensus that it would be a small taproom after attending the 2016 Craft Brewers Conference.

Tanks at Pantown Brewing in St. Cloud. The equipment was previously used by former St. Cloud breweries O'Hara's, McCann's and Lupine. *Courtesy of Andrew Webster.*

Czech and Johnson both wanted to hire an experienced professional brewer. They searched for about a year before settling on Nick Flies, who had previously brewed at other operations in the Twin Cities. After about a year of construction, Pantown Brewing debuted with four beers on tap: 1917 American IPA, Classic Cream Ale, Flat Iron Amber Ale and Drop Forge Milk Stout. The taproom features a bar top that was built by Czech and decorated with images of Pantown and the Pan Motor Co.

9

ST. JOSEPH MAKES BEER AND HARD CIDER

St. Joseph has always been known for its ties to the Catholic Church. Now, it is known for the fresh beer and cider made at its local brewery and cidery. The town, located less than ten miles west of St. Cloud, had originally been named Clinton, but its name was changed when the town church was built in 1870. For more than a century, St. Joseph has housed St. Benedict's Monastery and the College of St. Benedict. Nearby is century-old St. John's Abbey and St. John's University. People used to make pilgrimages to St. Joseph to see the grave of Moorhead-born Sister Annella Zervas, who died from a rare skin condition when she was just twenty-six years old. Later, people crowded the area to watch the national championship–winning St. John's football team and its longtime coach John Gagliardi—who was recognized as the all-time winningest head coach in college football history. Every Fourth of July, St. Joseph Catholic Church hosts a Joetown Rocks concert that attracts thousands and offers the specially seasoned and trademarked Joe Burgers.

Today, people make pilgrimages to St. Joseph for many of the same reasons that they always have, but there are two new reasons for people to visit. The artful town, with a population of fewer than ten thousand people, is home to both Bad Habit Brewing and Milk & Honey Ciders. The St. Joseph brewery and hard cidery are located about two miles apart and have innovated fermented alcohol in Central Minnesota and throughout the state. Both introduced the taproom culture to St. Joseph and have regularly drawn large crowds of residents and visitors.

St. Joseph had little brewing history until recently. In 1870, Louis Brinks founded a brewery in the town, along the Sauk River, and he used a Dutch-style windmill to grind the grains. However, Brinks was arrested for illegally distilling in November 1872. Brinks sold the St. Joseph brewery in 1875 and ran another brewery in Frazee City until 1879. The St. Joseph brewery burned down in 1881 and was never rebuilt

Elsewhere in the Twin Cities, former St. John's national championship football players went on to form Fulton Brewing. The operation, which is known for its Sweet Child of Vine IPA, has become one of the state's largest breweries and has a taproom just down the street from the Minnesota Twins' home, Target Field. The founders even got their former coach, the late John Gagliardi, to sample some of their brews before he passed away at the age of ninety-one in 2018. The founders of Fulton Brewing say Gagliardi's wise lessons and words of wisdom helped them build their business.

Bad Habit Brewing

Forklifts carried Bad Habit Brewing's equipment less than six hundred feet across a St. Joseph street in the spring of 2019. The brewery that had been launched with an intimate, fifty-person Halloween party in 2015 had already outgrown its original space. The expansion was necessary to keep up with popular demand. Bad Habit quickly developed as a cult favorite among Minnesota's craft beer geeks. Like many Central Minnesota locations, it became a popular pit stop for both locals and tourists to the Twin Cities during the summer. Bad Habit had also emerged as a centerpiece and trademark of the historically small community. The brewery, with a catchy trademark slogan of "Be Good, Drink Bad," helped give the town its own beer identity in Central Minnesota. Bad Habit gave St. Joseph a watering hole that was able to be frequented by families, and it has become one of the most successful community breweries that spawned in Minnesota after the passage of the Surly Bill.

Bad Habit's new space in an old bank and city hall building has given the brewery more than twice the capacity of its original space; it has an outdoor patio area that allows for lounging and the opportunity to brew more beer. The brewery's opening day in May 2019 brought a full house of guests interested in seeing the new digs. Bad Habit's space was designed with a classic, industrial look in mind. An old bank safe serves as its walk-

A beer at Bad Habit Brewing in St. Joseph. *Courtesy of Andrew Webster.*

in cooler; when you open the door, your senses are struck with the dank aroma of hops. A two-hundred-person patio was built as a space for playing games and lounging on gorgeous summer and fall Minnesota days. A garage door opens up the main taproom on those days as well. Board games are played by patrons throughout the bar area, and a private room is available for large parties. Customers can practice their tap pouring skills at the taproom's water station. This location also has more parking spaces and larger bathrooms than the original spot. The brewing space has expanded to include more equipment, and a basement allows Bad Habit to experiment with barrel-aging.

The concept of Bad Habit Brewing had been in the back of founder Aaron Rieland's mind for at least a decade before the father of three actually opened the brewery in 2015. Shortly after the new millennium, Rieland found a homebrew kit for sale and thought that the idea of making his own beer was intriguing. He purchased a simple blonde golden ale kit and brewed it up—his enthusiasm waned once he tried the finished product. "It was terrible," Rieland joked. "So, I kind of gave up on homebrewing for about five years...until I was cleaning out the attic one day and found the kit. I

Bad Habit Brewing co-owner Eric Geier pours a beer at the St. Joseph taproom. *Courtesy of Andrew Webster.*

The chalkboard menu at Bad Habit Brewing in St. Joseph. *Courtesy of Andrew Webster.*

figured I should try it again." Rieland said he followed the instructions more closely in his second attempt and found better results. His beers continued to improve in the following batches.

Rieland progressed to all-grain brewing; he and a friend ramped up production and began brewing together about four times a month—most often in Rieland's home garage. Rieland began winning homebrew competition medals, and all the while, he planned brewery pit stops on family trips around the country. Rieland tried different beer styles while his children enjoyed root beers and the laid-back atmosphere of brewery culture. Rieland began thinking about bringing some of that culture to St. Cloud and started scouting locations in St. Cloud in 2013. Briefly, his realtor was Beaver Island co-founder Matt Studer. The two discussed partnering on a project at a lunch meeting before they later decided to pursue separate ventures. Rieland also toured potential brewery locations in the St. Cloud suburbs of Waite Park and Sartell. Then, an opportunity arose in St. Joseph.

Rieland initially agreed to be a part of a St. Joseph development that included another restaurant and housing space. When the project stalled to lock in a restaurant partner, Rieland nearly dropped the project. But he ultimately found a vacant space a block away at 15 East Minnesota Street. He purchased a five-barrel commercial system and began scaling up his homebrew recipes. Rieland's intention was to constantly rotate in new recipes by keeping his production to small batches. Bad Habit Brewing was chosen as the brewery's name as an ode to Rieland's garage homebrewing—which his family jokingly referred to as his "bad habit." He spent several months expanding the original brewery.

Bad Habit was initially opened as a weekend experiment; the taproom debuted with only Friday and Saturday hours, and a chocolate milk stout, India pale ale, saison and cream ale were among the first beers it produced. While Rieland was confident in his beers, he wasn't entirely sure that a brewery could thrive in such a small community—there was little craft beer available in St. Joseph at the time. Rieland initially kept his full-time job with a St. Cloud water treatment company. He credits his family's support during this time as the key to the brewery's success. He brewed new batches of beer after work during the week, which made for many long hours.

Rieland introduced craft beer to a number of locals. Bad Habit was one of the first Central Minnesota breweries to make sour beers and hazy IPAs. The brewery's original chocolate milk stout, Dark Addiction, has become one of its best-selling beers, and it has become the signature beer of the operation. Bad Habit continues to make small batches of experimental beers

Right: A beer at Bad Habit Brewing in St. Joseph. *Courtesy of Andrew Webster.*

Below: Colorful crowler cans at Bad Habit Brewing in St. Joseph. *Courtesy of Andrew Webster.*

Brewing tanks at Bad Habit Brewing in St. Joseph. *Courtesy of Andrew Webster.*

Tap handles at Bad Habit Brewing in St. Joseph. *Courtesy of Andrew Webster.*

A variety of crowlers at Bad Habit Brewing in St. Joseph. *Courtesy of Andrew Webster.*

that typically only stay on tap for a few days. About six months after Bad Habit first opened its doors to the public, the business was so successful—beyond Rieland's expectations—that he was able to leave his full-time job and focus exclusively on the brewery. Bad Habit expanded its hours beyond Friday and Saturday, and a crowler machine was later added to accompany the brewery's popular growler sales.

Eric Geier joined Rieland as a co-owner and the brewery's first full-time employee. The two have since become notorious for their viral Facebook videos of the shenanigans at the brewery. "We have a crazy sense of humor," Rieland said. Geier, a St. John's University graduate, first made home wines and ciders before attempting homebrewing. He currently lives in Cold Spring with his family.

One of the first people to check out Bad Habit's beer was the brewery's future brewmaster, Erik Salmi. According to a 2017 *St. Cloud Times* article, Salmi had been a St. Cloud teacher until his position was cut by the school district in 2009. Salmi then, unexpectedly, found a new career in brewing. He moved to Corvallis, Oregon, the summer after his position was cut in order to be closer to his mother, who had just been diagnosed with breast cancer. While visiting, he became friends with the owner of a brewery called Block 15. Salmi was then hired to wash kegs a few nights a week. A few months later, an assistant brewer at Block 15 left, and Salmi was promoted to the position, where he learned brewing techniques on the job. Salmi then took a position at Town Hall Brewery in Minneapolis. Since its opening in 1997, the brewpub has long been a staple of Minnesota's brewing scene; it owns the most Great American Beer Festival medals of any Minnesota brewery. The establishment was one of the state's first breweries to craft barrel-aged beers. There, Salmi progressed to lead Town Hall's famed barrel-aging program, where he worked under revered Minnesota head brewer Mike Hoops. Salmi had a great job at Town Hall but was commuting daily from Central Minnesota. Then, Salmi and Rieland's wives met at a Central Minnesota "women in beer" event. Around this time, Rieland had decided that he needed to hire an experienced head brewer to take Bad Habit to the next level. Salmi had been impressed with the Bad Habit beers he had tried, and a new partnership eventually formed.

Bad Habit moved into its new space in 2019. The taproom hosts various events, and gradual growth is planned. At the time of this writing, the brewery has already become a staple of the storied St. Joseph community.

MILK & HONEY CIDERS

Apple trees cover a ten-acre portion of land on the edge of St. Joseph's downtown area; a patio campfire burns on perfect evenings, and a tasting room called Milk & Honey Ciders sits in the center of it all. The fruit throughout the property was strategically planted to be used in making hard ciders and to educate customers. The location was picked as it showcases rural cider making but is still easy for customers to drive to. The operation is meant to be a throwback to pre-Prohibition time, when American consumers enjoyed hard cider as much as they enjoyed beer. Historians even theorize that hard apple cider was likely enjoyed at the first Thanksgiving; during Prohibition, however, many storied cider farms were vacated, and the industry never fully recovered. The Milk & Honey Ciders taproom opened in summer of 2018 and hosts a full schedule of cheese pairing and food truck events. Locals were invited to the taproom's soft opening, where they went through one hundred gallons of hard cider on the first night.

The Milk & Honey Ciders taproom in St. Joseph. *Courtesy of Andrew Webster.*

A hard cider made from a variety of fermented apples at the Milk & Honey Ciders taproom in St. Joseph. *Courtesy of Andrew Webster.*

The Milk & Honey Ciders taproom in St. Joseph on a winter day. *Courtesy of Andrew Webster.*

Milk & Honey Ciders has been on tap in the Twin Cities since 2014. The vision of the craft hard cidery was first plotted out in 2011 by a trio of friends. Co-founder Peter Gillitzer handles the physical cidery of Milk & Honey; the ROCORI High School graduate obtained his master's degree in applied plant science from the University of Minnesota. Gillitzer grows specific apple cider varieties on his massive Cold Spring farm along the north bay of Byer Lake. Co-founder Adam Theis, another ROCORI graduate, brings professional brewing experience to the operation. Before Milk & Honey, Theis brewed professionally for Third Street Brewhouse of Cold Spring and Town Hall Brewery and Indeed Brewing Co. of Minneapolis. Theis also attended the prestigious Siebel Institute of Technology and World Brewing Academy. Co-founder Aaron Klocker is the engineer of the group and often manages the apple press. He comes from the aviation industry.

The trio decided to name their operation Milk & Honey Ciders—although there isn't any milk or honey in their products. Theis explained the name to the *St. Cloud Times*: "The general saying is the land of milk and honey is where everything is bountiful and good." Because it takes years to mature

The bar top at the Milk & Honey Ciders taproom in St. Joseph. *Courtesy of Andrew Webster.*

Tap handles at the Milk & Honey Ciders taproom in St. Joseph. *Courtesy of Andrew Webster.*

Left: A hard cider at the Milk & Honey Ciders taproom in St. Joseph. *Courtesy of Andrew Webster.*

Below: Employees ferment apple cider at the Milk & Honey Ciders taproom in St. Joseph. *Courtesy of Andrew Webster.*

a cider apple tree, Milk & Honey first launched its hard cidery by using cider apples that were sourced from elsewhere in Minnesota, Michigan, California, the Pacific Northwest and other locations throughout the New England region. The fruit was pressed and fermented on Gillitzer's Cold Spring property, and a special, commercially inspected building was added to house the product.

Milk & Honey uses heirloom and traditional cider apple varieties—these aren't like ones available in supermarkets. Cider apples are a bit smaller and are not grown to look attractive on market shelves. Instead, these apples are grown for flavor and character. Milk & Honey's products have a drier taste and are made in the traditional way. The hard cidery initially only distributed kegs to Twin Cities locations, but it later distributed to locations throughout Central Minnesota. Next, Milk & Honey four-packs became available in liquor stores throughout the state. Milk & Honey regularly pours at events throughout the state and is a fixture at the St. Cloud Ciderfest celebration every September. The business frequently educates the public on hard apple ciders and their histories. Milk & Honey is just one of more than a dozen cideries in the Minnesota Cider Guild.

The founders of Milk & Honey had always planned to add a taproom. When the business was first launched, the hard cidery had a small six-seat tasting room built into Gillitzer's home. Access to the tasting room could only be gained by invitation. Gillitzer knew a public taproom would have to be located elsewhere—even if he did want it at his house, the location was a bit difficult for customers to get to. Instead, the trio found a ten-acre site at the edge of St. Joseph. There, they fulfilled their visions of building a cider land of milk and honey that gave an ode to one of America's favorite drinks.

10

CLOUDY TOWN BREWERS AND ST. CLOUD'S BEER GUY

Guest Chapter by longtime St. Cloud Times *Beer Guy and Homebrew Pioneer Bruce LeBlanc*

Cloudy Town Brewers and the Local Beer Guy

When Bruce LeBlanc goes out on the town, people often tell him he looks familiar. They just often can't remember exactly from where. LeBlanc and his column photo have run regularly in the St. Cloud Times *newspaper since the early 2000s. LeBlanc has penned a weekly beer pick series that has earned him the nickname of the Central Minnesota "Beer Guy." The Sauk Rapids resident has lived in the area his whole life. The craft beer lover helped pioneer homebrewing in the area with the Cloudy Town Brewers. He's a certified beer judge and has kept fellow beer aficionados of the area informed with his reviews. LeBlanc has kindly agreed to share the history of one of the area's premier homebrew clubs with this guest chapter.*

Back in the early 1980s, a friend gave me a beer from a new brewery in Minnesota, a Summit Extra Pale Ale. This was my first taste of real craft beer. One sip and I knew that the days of the yellow fizzy stuff were coming to an end for me. As more craft beers slowly came about from the likes of August Schell's, Summit and Cold Spring Export—to name a few—I knew that I wanted to try making this tasty brew myself. Trouble is, the information and ingredients out there were very limited. Central Minnesota had the Baker's Craft & Hobby store that had a few beer kits and some supplies, but everything to do with homebrewing was limited back then.

A while later, a friend of mine gave me a homebrew kit that he had received as a wedding gift. The stigma of brewing alcohol products forced his new wife to make him get rid of the kit. So, he gave the kit to me—bulging, swelling cans of extract and all. I could not wait to give it a try. As one might expect, it came out less than perfect, but the fire had been lit. I kept brewing with less than favorable results, but I fell in love with the whole process. One day, I came across an advertisement about homebrewing classes at Brew & Grow, a homebrew supplier in Minneapolis. I signed right up, drove down to Minneapolis and took the class. It was very helpful, and with a few tweaks to my process, everything improved greatly. Who knew you shouldn't leave steaming hot wort outside, uncovered, overnight to cool?

Folks like me had heard of homebrew clubs, but there were none in Central Minnesota at the time. That's when another short-lived homebrew store came along in the early 1990s called Shirt Tails. They were in a rented space inside the Sauk Rapids, Minnesota Municipal Liquor Store, and they were all about homebrewing. The fellow who ran Shirt Tails—I do not recall his name—tried to start a homebrew club. I went to the one and only meeting he had, but he came into a medical condition and had to disband the store and the idea of a homebrew club. A few more years went by with no network of homebrew friends. The hobby was still in its infancy, and that certainly was the case in Central Minnesota—this was long before things like the internet were common. Then, another fellow by the name of Greg Koob started a German restaurant in downtown St. Cloud, Minnesota, that featured Minnesota-made beers only. He was the one who pursued the idea of a homebrew club in Central Minnesota. He started having meetings with the local homebrewers, and the Cloudy Town Brewers homebrew club was born.

The first years' worth of meetings consisted of a handful of people showing up and discussing and sampling their liquid creations. A lot of other issues were discussed, including what the structure of the meetings should be and whether or not the club should have a formal structure and rules. I found discussions of that nature to be uninteresting, and I began to drift a bit. Then, one day, I received a call from Greg; he congratulated me on being elected as the president of the club. I was a bit shocked. I did not know I was running for president. What am I supposed to do as a president? Am I supposed to talk in front of people when we have meetings? I've never done this before—I am just a homebrewer. But things worked out, and our club was growing.

Charlie Papazian, the founder of the American Homebrewers Association, has a motto: relax, don't worry, have a homebrew. I have incorporated that into my approach of running the Cloudy Town Brewers and, well, my approach to everything in life. The club meetings should be low-key and fun, yet informative; that is my style. Slowly, the meetings grew in attendance. We started having club competitions at meetings that featured one style of beer in order to learn more about that style. In the summers, we had beer picnics and meetings in local parks—that is, the parks that would allow us, as beer-themed gatherings were still frowned upon in those days. We started a homebrew newsletter called the *Clarifier* that came out every month with information on homebrewing and meeting locations. We started venturing out to different locations for meetings. In the early days, it was difficult to find meeting locations; we usually went to bars, but many were apprehensive to have us because we brought in homebrew to sample. As they realized that we usually ordered food and the craft beers they had—and that the sampling of our homebrews was just a minor part of the night—they became friendlier.

Back then, very few Minnesota craft beers were available; you had Summit, August Schell's, James Paige and Cold Spring Export. You could find European lagers in the import section at beer stores, but they usually came in green bottles. Because shelf space and refrigeration were usually reserved for the mega brews, most imports were stored warm, on the shelves under artificial lighting, and you know what that does to beer. There was a time that I was at a liquor store picking up some brews, and the fellow in front of me at the checkout counter inquired about one of the import lagers sitting on the shelf in a warm green bottle. The salesperson said, "Oh yeah, that's a good beer. It has that tasty, skunky import flavor." We were all lucky that I was pressed for time, because I was ready to give a lecture on proper beer flavors and storage, and who knows how long that would have taken.

Homebrew Campouts

One activity that is great fun is the Minnesota homebrewers' campout. The campout is open to all homebrew clubs, statewide, and pretty much anyone who is a beer enthusiast. The one thing about the homebrew community is that we're very inclusive; the only thing you must be is a beer enthusiast, and you're welcome. The campout is sponsored by a different Minnesota homebrew club each year. They pick the location, put on a feast for Saturday evening and run the campout homebrew contest.

Everyone at the campout is easy to get along with, and the beer selection is the best in the state. Many kegged homebrews are on tap at the campout and are free for all to try. There are dozens of tasty brews to choose from. In the evenings, there is a campfire, where campers will break out those special, rare and hard-to-find beers, ciders and meads from all over the country. They open the bottle, pour themselves a sample and pass it on. The samples keep coming in a complete delight for the palate. As the night wears on and people loosen up a bit, someone usually breaks out a guitar and starts singing around the campfire.

The campout competition takes place on Saturday afternoon and is held to just a few styles of beer. The winner gets a traveling trophy, which they hold for a year until the next campout. The Saturday evening feast is a treat for the taste buds. The cuisine is not your average campout food; it can be themed—internationally or regionally—or it could just be a culinary treat that someone is good at making. One time, we even had a pig roast. The food is always something special, and there's plenty to eat. It's a feast that will prep you for another night around the campfire. The campout is a laid-back event where people can come and go as they please, take naps or socialize when they want and where there are plenty of good beers to sample. This event is the highlight of the summer.

Educating the public on the merits of craft and homebrewing has always been part of Cloudy Town Brewers' philosophy. We have done community education at one of the area's junior high schools in the past, and we have brewed more beer in that public school than one might believe. Many a good laugh was had while giving these demonstrations in a home economics classroom. One time, a college student took the class and asked us during the demonstration if it was true that beer can give you a beer belly; I replied that I have drunk many brews in my time, and I did not think it had a great effect. She replied, "You have potential." My partners just about fell over laughing at that comment—it's all in good fun. For a while, we were doing brewing demonstrations at the Benton County Fair. We did all-grain and extract brewing methods outdoors at the fair. We had great fun talking with people and demonstrating the merits of homebrewing. Many old-timers would come by and see the homemade copper coiled wort chiller we were using and would say, "I know what you're up to with that." I had to tell them that we were not making moonshine, just beer.

It is always fun to brew with different people at these events. Some folks are very technical and break out digital scales and thermometers, referencing charts and tables in books. I tend not to get too technical, especially when doing demonstrations. I keep it simple—just grab a handful of hops and throw them in the kettle. Relax, don't worry, have a homebrew. One time, we were at the fair doing outdoor brewing demonstrations under an oak tree, when a splash came from my brew kettle. A fellow homebrewer said that he had seen an acorn drop into the kettle. No problem, it should float, right? Wrong; acorns do not float in brew kettles. Because of space constraints, we could not move to another spot. By the time the boil was over, there were over a dozen acorns in the beer. Don't worry, relax, have a homebrew; the beer turned out fine. I believe this is where aging beer in oak got its primitive start.

The Cloudy Town Brewers also host a technical night for members. Once a month, interested members get together and have in-depth discussions on brewing processes, procedures and beer styles. These gatherings really increase members' knowledge of beer and brewing. The more you know, the better your homebrew.

Around 1999, the Cloudy Town Brewers thought it should step it up a bit and hold a BJCP (beer judge certification program)-sanctioned homebrew competition. These events are open to homebrewers nationwide. The first few times we held a competition, it was a huge undertaking. All aspects of BJCP-sanctioned competitions have very specific standards for legitimacy. Advertising the event required a lot of organization, and finding sponsors and certified judges to judge the event was difficult. Back then, there was only one recognized judge in our area; certified judges who had taken the Beer Judge Certification Program in the state were limited, as it was a really new concept back then. With all of the categories of beer that needed to be judged, we needed as many judges as we could get.

With a lot of tenacity, the event finally came together. It was held at the original Granite City Food & Brew. These homebrew contests normally have a guest judge panel of celebrity and nationally ranked judges for the Best of the Show beers, and because of our connections with Granite City Food & Brew and their connections with the craft beer world, we landed the most famous man of beer: author Michael Jackson, the original "Beer Hunter" from England. Michael Jackson was an author who traveled the world, visiting breweries, old and new, and writing about all beer styles and the brewing techniques of yore. If you want to learn about beer, Michael Jackson's books are a must. With the addition of Michael Jackson, our Best of Show judging panel was complete and very respectable. It was an honor to chat with Michael Jackson at our first sanctioned homebrew contest—what a great start.

March Mashness is an annual event, where we invite anyone who is interested in homebrewing to participate. It is an educational event, and whether or not you submit a brew to be judged, you get feedback about your brew from certified judges. To help steward and judge the event, we always invite folks who are interested to sit in on judging panels and give it a try. It's like a crash course on beer styles, brewing techniques, flaws and the process of judging. The judges will walk you through the process in a welcoming way—there's no need to be intimidated.

The first few years we held March Mashness, it was very difficult to find certified judges for the event. There were not many judges in the state at that time, and we needed almost every judge in the state to travel here to help make our event successful. Finally, after an event of what I like to call "judge abuse," or making judges judge as many sessions as possible with extensive palate fatigue, we decided to hold our first BJCP classes for becoming a certified judge. For those of you who think that this sounds simple and fun, let me inform you, it's no simple task. The learning process can be fun, but it's very intense. In my day job, which is totally different from the beer world, I have a chief engineer's license that took years of work experience and a lot of testing to attain—the final exam was quite intense. But if you ask me which test was harder, I would have to say the BJCP exam was harder. You basically take beer and brewing down to the molecular level and build your understanding up from there. Back then, the test had very little true-or-false or multiple-choice type questions; it was mostly composed of timed essay questions—no easy task. After our initial exam, we were all exhausted, and our brains felt numb from the test. But we persevered, and there are now quite a few BJCP-certified judges in our area, which makes judging March Mashness much easier and a much more pleasant experience, overall.

A pleasant result of the Cloudy Town Brewers are our professional brewer "alumni." We have several Cloudy Town Brewers who have taken their hobby and turned it into a trade. We have had members who went on to brew for Third Street Brewhouse in Cold Spring, Beaver Island Brewing in St. Cloud, Lake Superior Brewing in Duluth and Boat House

Brewing in Eli. Patrick Sunberg started Jack Pine, the Brainerd area's first brewery since Prohibition called, and since starting the brewery, it became so popular that he had to expand. He built a beautiful new brewery with more capacity and ambiance. Hard work does pay off.

One of the special attributes of the homebrew and craft brew community is its comradery and how its members support each other. Do you need a sponsor for your homebrew competition? The local breweries are sure to help out. Do you have an award-winning homebrew and want to share the recipe? That's not a problem; we share all of the information about our beers and how we brew them. There are always plenty of Cloudy Town Brewers willing to share information on beer styles and brewing techniques. One time, I was at a brewery, chatting with the brewers, and I referred to another brewery as their competition. I was immediately corrected, and they said that they do not see others as competition but as friends in the craft beer community who support each other in the endeavor of making better beer. That really is the way it should be.

In the early 2000s, the *St. Cloud Times* approached the Cloudy Town Brewers and said that it would like to do a weekly beer review called "Local Beer Pick of the Week" and wanted to know if we would like to do it. I do not recall if I volunteered or was nominated for the job—or a combination of both—but I got the job of writing a weekly beer review for the paper. It was a bit challenging at first; there were only a handful of breweries in the state, and there just was not a lot of selection at the time, but that sure has changed. I grew to enjoy my "research," sampling new beers and writing about them. Now, over fifteen years later, I have written over seven hundred reviews. The reviews offer a little information on the brewery, where it came from and maybe a little background on its style. I also write a positive opinion of the beer itself. The reviews can help readers make a better choice when they see a beer on the shelf at the store or a taproom. With so many breweries and beer styles out there, they may not really know what they're getting into and whether they will like a certain style or not. Plus, craft beers are more expensive than macros, and it helps to make a more educated choice when purchasing them.

A recent development in Central Minnesota is the St. Cloud Craft Beer Tour, which takes place in January, and Ciderfest, which takes place in late summer. At these events, participants can sample hundreds of different beers and ciders. It is a complete joy to participate in these events and witness the public's growing enthusiasm for craft beer. Thousands of people attend these events, and it is refreshing to witness the continued growth of the industry. Cloudy Town Brewers helps out by volunteering at these, and we now have a booth at these events, where we distribute information on homebrewing and share samples of our homebrews.

So, there you have it—an enlightened view of craft beer and homebrewing in Central Minnesota from my perspective. It has been incredible to watch the brew world grow around us. Thousands of people are now employed in the industry in Minnesota, which, just ten or so years ago, employed only a fraction of the people it does now. For me, it has been a long, fun ride that I hope continues for some time to come. We have a vibrant beer community here that we all have made many good friends from. Cheers!

11

HOMEBREW CLUB SPAWNS LUPULIN, SPILLED GRAIN

Three Minnesota community craft breweries share the same humble roots. The founders of Big Lake's Lupulin Brewing, Annandale's Spilled Grain Brewhouse and Hutchinson's Bobbing Bobber Brewery learned the art and science of brewing together in homebrew club meetings. The Wright County–based group began meeting in 2009. The members of the homebrew club were initially more focused on having an excuse to drink beer than perfecting their homebrew recipes, but as the group evolved and new members joined, more attention was given to the cleanliness of their beers and improving their final results. The group explored different beer styles together. A healthy competition emerged among club members to see who could medal higher at homebrew competitions—members of the group have a wide collection of homebrew medals to their credit. Wright County is the state's tenth-largest county, but it had little brewing history, even before Prohibition. But the area eventually fostered the state's future craft beer expansion craze.

When the Surly Bill was passed in 2011, the advanced members of the Wright County homebrew group took notice. The ability for a brewery to have its own taproom allowed smaller Minnesota cities to get in on the craft beer revolution; a taproom model took less capital to start, and it brought in an immediate cash flow that had been prevented since Prohibition. While the members of the Wright County Homebrew Club had competed against each other, they only ever aided each other in launching their breweries. While Lupulin, Spilled Grain and Bobbing Bobber are their own businesses, the founders consulted and modeled their operations after each other's businesses. The group that was started as an excuse to drink beer gave three Minnesota communities and plenty of tourists their own excuse to drink beer.

Lupulin Brewing

Located just off Highway 10, in the heart of Big Lake, is one of the state's most successful community breweries. Lupulin Brewing has become a destination for Big Lake residents, cabin traffic and Minnesota craft beer geeks. The brewery, which was opened in 2015, had two major expansions within its first five years of operating. Lupulin Brewing was recognized by the Brewers Association for being one of the country's fifty fastest-growing operations. Their motto of "Work sucks, drink beer" has resonated with beer drinkers. Lupulin is named after a yellow hop plant powder and has become best known for its IPAs, namely its hazy version called Hooey. Lupulin's co-founders, Jeff Zierdt of Monticello and Matt Schiller of Montrose, had reconnected with each other in the homebrew club. They were first acquainted in Wisconsin Rapids, where Schiller grew up and Zierdt worked at a paper mill for more than two decades. Years later, they had the same vision for Lupulin Brewing and made it a reality together.

Schiller became obsessed with craft beer shortly after turning twenty-one, and he discovered more sophisticated beer when he sampled beer at St. Paul's brewpub Great Waters Brewing. The brewery, which specialized in cask ales, was opened in 1997 and was the oldest operating brewpub in Minnesota's capital city before it closed in November 2018. Later, Schiller was invited to homebrew with a co-worker; he went over to his house and assisted with a traditional kit beer. Schiller became so obsessed with this new beer-making hobby that he quickly purchased an all-grain brewing system. His first solo homebrew on the system was so bad that Schiller had to dump it, but the perfectionist went on to win a second-place medal in a St. Cloud homebrew competition with his third-ever batch. Schiller won the contest with an original recipe that he had crafted himself.

Schiller joined the Wright County Homebrew Club in 2010, and he quickly became the group's education director. Schiller emphasized sanitation in the beer-making process and used his role as an excuse to endlessly study brewing and beer styles. He taught the group about brewing certain styles, and then everyone would brew that beer; at the next meeting, they sampled and discussed their results.

Zierdt also joined the Wright County Homebrew Club in 2010. He had been gifted an extract homebrew kit from his wife and son, Aaron, on the previous Father's Day. He tried to make an amber ale and Irish red ale with the kits, but he ultimately became obsessed with stouts. Fortunately, a stout presentation was made at his first Wright County Homebrew Club meeting, and Schiller convinced Zierdt to upgrade to an all-grain system. Zierdt then began collecting numerous homebrew medals for his oatmeal stout recipe.

Schiller and Zierdt built a strong bond over beer. The two fantasized about opening their own brewery and formalized the LLC in May 2012. Nearly three years later, the operation known as Lupulin Brewing was opened. Schiller and Zierdt didn't initially target Big Lake, but it was in the region where they were to start a business. Research showed that a brewery desert existed north of Highway 55, south of Highway 10 and west of 494. They first looked at locations near the Albertville Mall and later presented their proposal to officials in Hanover and Monticello. Then, an advertising consultant who had been helping Schiller and Zierdt recommended Big Lake—she was a high school friend of the town's mayor. Big Lake had rejected big box stores in favor of more community-owned businesses, something that attracted the duo. Big Lake courted the brewery, and a lease was signed for a strip mall space right off Highway 10 in April 2014. According to Schiller's and Zierdt's research, Lupulin Brewing was Big Lake's first-ever commercial brewery.

The Big Lake community was supportive of the brewery from the beginning but had plenty of questions about the craft beer at Lupulin. The brewery produced 330 barrels in 2015; its production grew to 1,606 by 2017 and more than double that in 2019. Lupulin was included in the Brewers Association's inaugural list of the "50 Fastest Growing Breweries" in the United States in 2018. Making the list brought legions of craft beer geeks to the taproom. Zierdt's son, Aaron, underwent formal brewing training in Europe and became co–head brewer at Lupulin. Aaron specializes in brewing small-batch beers.

The owners of Lupulin always planned for it to be a hop-forward brewery. Its beer schedule was launched with a rotating experimental IPA called the Blissful Ignorance series. The fourth addition was a double IPA that was conditioned with a heavy dosage of citra, mosaic and columbus hops. The beer was so popular that it became a year-round beer simply known as Blissful Ignorance. Lupulin later released a hazy IPA called Hooey that has been its top seller ever since. Lupulin is also known for its Belgian blonde, which has been on the menu since the brewery debuted, and a coffee stout called Javatized. Every year, Lupulin makes a potato kolsch beer for Big Lake's Spudfest festival. In 2017, Lupulin won a gold medal at the prestigious Great American Beer Festival in the German-style Oktoberfest division for its Dortmunder. When the medal was awarded, Lupulin only had a keg left of the beer. It is now highly sought after by beer geeks when it's released every fall.

Lupulin entered a new era in 2019, when the facility got a $4 million expansion. The first brewery to spawn from the Wright County Homebrew Club has not only become a template for other members, but it has become an inspiration for aspiring breweries across the country.

Spilled Grain Brewhouse

Brewing beer had long been a hobby of Jacob Schnabel when he took a second job as the head brewer at Spilled Grain Brewhouse. The St. Cloud Cathedral High School graduate had fourteen years of homebrew experience, a closet full of homebrew competition medals and a successful job as an engineer—not to mention a wife and kids at home. Schnabel was originally inspired by Sam Adams Boston lager and honed his craft with the Wright County Homebrew Club. He soon became close with both Zierdt and Schiller; for the trio, homebrewing was more of a way of life than a hobby. Much of his engineering expertise came in handy when homebrewing. Other members of the beer industry with engineering backgrounds, like Fat Tire creator Jeff Lebesch, have translated their knowledge to the brewing success throughout the industry.

Schnabel was initially recruited to be the head brewer and to brew twice a week, but he ultimately became the leader of the project. He started with a three-and-a-half-barrel system but has since upgraded. Schnabel has continued to win brewing medals, now at the national level, and Spilled Grain displays his accomplishments in its taproom. Like most other Central Minnesota breweries, Spilled Grain has a crowd of both regulars and cabin traffic during every summer.

Tap handles at Spilled Grain Brewhouse in Annandale. *Courtesy of Andrew Webster.*

Spilled Grain was named for Schnabel's original brewery business partner, co-founder Dan Seaberg, who grew up in Annandale. His memory of piles of spilled grain from when he was an eight-year-old in the town is still vivid to him. Seaberg was playing when the sound of a large crash echoed through the sky, and a dust cloud drifted in from the distance. Seaberg investigated the scene and found derailed trains and huge piles of grain lying on top of the tracks. Years later, Spilled Grain would be the name of a brewery that cleverly fit both the brewery and history of Annandale. Seaberg also brought his family's history of brewing into the business. His great-grandfather had been a brewer in Germany before immigrating to Joliet, Illinois. Seaberg briefly revived the family tradition but has since gone on to other business ventures.

Spilled Grain, meanwhile, has become a hub for the Annandale community, hosting events and concerts at the taproom, which is located just off Highway 55. Its beers are also on tap throughout the city located southwest of St. Cloud. Annandale has long been a city with frequent

The bar top at Spilled Grain Brewhouse in Annandale. *Courtesy of Andrew Webster.*

Taproom seating at Spilled Grain Brewhouse in Annandale. *Courtesy of Andrew Webster.*

A beer at Spilled Grain Brewhouse in Annandale. *Courtesy of Andrew Webster.*

Beer competition medals at Spilled Grain Brewhouse in Annadale. Courtesy of Andrew Webster.

The bar top at Spilled Grain Brewhouse in Annandale. *Courtesy of Andrew Webster.*

The brewing equipment at Spilled Grain Brewhouse in Annandale. *Courtesy of Andrew Webster.*

Stacks of grain and supplies at Spilled Grain Brewhouse in Annandale. *Courtesy of Andrew Webster.*

A wide view of the taproom at Spilled Grain Brewhouse in Annandale. *Courtesy of Andrew Webster.*

Taproom seating at Spilled Grain Brewhouse in Annandale. *Courtesy of Andrew Webster.*

visitors. Known as the "Heart of the Lakes," Annandale has twenty-six lakes within a ten-mile radius, which keeps a steady influx of travelers in search of boating and fishing. Annandale has long only had a couple thousand residents. "It's really a great place to live," Schnabel said. "The town has been fantastic [to watch] grow in appreciation for craft beer."

Before Spilled Grain opened its doors in July 2015, Annandale had little craft beer on tap. The few bars that did exist prior to Spilled Grain primarily served the core domestic brands. Research shows that Spilled Grain was Annandale's first-ever commercial brewery, even before Prohibition. A light but flavorful cream ale has become the main introduction of craft beer to the Annandale community. Spilled Grain's Kinnikinnick Kream won a gold medal at the U.S. Open Beer Championships and a bronze at the 2018 North American Beer Awards.

The Annandale community has been treated to a well-recognized selection of beers. Spilled Grain won a gold medal at the 2018 U.S. Beer Open for its Old Ale and a silver medal at the 2017 U.S. Beer Open for its doppelbock called Emancipator. Over the years, Spilled Grain has collected bronze medals at the U.S. Beer Open for its Oktoberfest and

A beer at Spilled Grain Brewhouse in Annandale. *Courtesy of Andrew Webster.*

old ale called Bearded Man. Its American-style IPA called Highest Point has also become a popular beer. Spilled Grain named its flagship stout Bungalow Island after the island located in the middle of an Annandale area's chain of lakes. Schnabel has also experimented with single-malt and single-hop beers.

As Spilled Grain and Lupulin have found success, its founders haven't forgotten their roots. At the end of their first calendar year of business, in December 2015, the breweries made their first collaboration beers together. Schiller came to Annandale for the first batch and Schnabel went to Lupulin two days later for the second batch. The creation was a 9.8-percent imperial India brown ale that was brewed like a brown ale and dry-hopped like an IPA. Schnabel oversaw the malt build, and Schiller scheduled the hop additions. The two breweries have remained connected as their operations have evolved.

Bobbing Bobber Brewery

The third brewery to emerge from the Wright County club is housed just outside Central Minnesota on Main Street in Hutchinson. Like Lupulin and Spilled Grain, the operation was set up in a smaller community of a city that didn't have a brewery. Hutchinson was founded in the 1800s by members of a harmonizing singing group called the Hutchinson Family Singers. Hutchinson has since become a manufacturing hub with a 3M plant.

Dan Hart opened Bobbing Bobber Brewing Company—also known as 3BC—with head brewer Lane Wanous in Hutchinson in May 2018. According to *Growler Magazine*, the taproom's opening broke a twenty-nine-mile brewery desert. Hart and Wanouse tapped into the experiences of Lupulin and Spilled Grain as they planned and built their brewery. Bobbing Bobber Brewing opened in Hutchinson's old Coca-Cola bottling plant, giving new life to the historic building. Hart had dreamed up the concept of Bobbing Bobber Brewery years before. The Mound, Minnesota native had worked in the restaurant and bar industry for a decade after attending Normandale Community College.

Hart's first plan was to start his own restaurant; then, he began homebrewing in 2009, and within four years, his family and friends suggested that he should open his own brewery. Hart, instead, shifted to a career of being a railroad conductor for eleven years. But Hart's experience in the service industry was still fresh in his mind when he changed his career focus to building a business around beer. He initially made plans to open a beer bar featuring brews made by various breweries, but he realized that the regulations around food and beer would be challenging. So, the project then transformed into a brewery and taproom. Hart came up with 3BC's clever and tongue-twisting name while out on a fishing boat. With his reel in the water and a homebrew in his hand, he realized that he'd gone hours without catching a fish—he had just been staring at a bobbing bobber in the water all day. Thus, the name Bobbing Bobber Brewing Company was born.

Wanous served as the head brewer of Bobbing Bobber Brewing. The Cokato native grew up on a dairy farm, dreaming of playing in the NHL and being a naval aviator. Wanous, instead, had a career as a welder and worked in quality control positions. He was gifted a homebrew kit one Christmas and became obsessed. He soon upgraded to all-grain brewing and began developing his own recipes. Bobbing Bobber Brewing debuted with a kolsch, cream ale, cream ale on cold press, honey wheat with orange blossom honey, honey wheat with raspberries, citra pale ale, gose, American red, Chinook IPA, porter and salted brown ale. Many of the beers are named after fishing terms, like the Crappie Flop IPA, Row Your Boat Robust Porter and Capsize Kolsch.

12

SURROUNDING BREWERIES

Taprooms began popping up throughout Minneapolis and St. Paul after the Surly Bill passed in 2011 and made it easier for Minnesotans to run breweries. The beer culture eventually spread out to smaller communities. While the first breweries that opened in smaller towns often questioned if their business could be sustained, many found success in the community brewery model. Not every brewery business venture in Central Minnesota has been successful, but breweries in Buffalo, Sauk Rapids, Little Falls and Monticello have spread craft beer throughout the area. For some communities, these were their first-ever breweries; for others, these breweries were revivals of past traditions. Each of them has introduced new craft beers to drinkers in their community. The following are the stories of Hayes Public House, Urban Lodge, Starry Eyed, Rustech and Nordic breweries.

Hayes Public House

One of Minnesota's first small communities to have its own craft beer taproom was Buffalo, on the edge of Buffalo Lake. Hayes Public House opened its doors in 2013 and became a template for fellow breweries that were looking to launch in smaller communities. The operation, which has since expanded multiple times, was frequently approached by city councils of other cities to learn how they could also attract a community brewery.

Hayes has won over beer drinkers from Buffalo and afar with its traditional Irish- and English-style creations—an Irish red and an Irish stout are among its most popular beers.

The vision for Hayes Public House first came from its founder, Pugs Hayes. He grew up in the service industry working at his grandmother's Stella's Café in Monticello, Minnesota. The restaurant was a community institution for three decades, run by the late Stella Schenieder, who was also a World War II veteran. Hayes first thought to start an Irish pub to carry on his family's restaurateur legacy. The self-proclaimed history buff told the *Growler Magazine* that he could trace his family genealogy to an early 1700s Scotch-Irish settlement in the Shenandoah Valley. Hayes's family later resettled in Delano, Minnesota. His vision of an Irish pub eventually evolved into a brewery.

He discovered homebrewing while he was a college student studying business. Like it has for most brewers, the hobby quickly became an obsession for Hayes. He started with extract kits before upgrading to an all-grain system. Hayes, being a certified welder, eventually built his own homebrew system, welding the parts himself. That very system has served as the pilot brewery for many of Hayes's beers on tap. Hayes initially looked for a brewery location in the city of Monticello, where Stella's Café had been such a big part of the community. But his target location quickly shifted to Buffalo, which was proactively trying to bring in a brewery. Historical records state that Hayes Public House was Buffalo's first-ever brewery. The location in the county seat was also Wright County's first commercial brewery since Prohibition—which meant that numerous local laws had to be navigated before Hayes Public House was able to open.

Buffalo was incorporated in May 1857 and was named after the 1,552-acre Buffalo Lake, which was named by native traders for its abundance of Buffalo fish. Buffalo Lake and Lake Pulaski, which rests on the other side of Buffalo, were used as a camping, fishing and hunting ground by the Sioux, or Dakota, tribe. According to city archives, the earliest European settlers in the area were fur traders who set up the first post on Lake Pulaski in the mid-1800s. At the time, the Buffalo area was heavily forested and known as the "Big Woods." The first settlers constructed log shacks, averaging around twelve-by-twenty feet in size. The resorts on Buffalo's lakes soon became popular tourist destinations.

Just like Buffalo has plenty of tradition, Hayes Public House has a number of its own brewing traditions. Hayes has primarily focused on creating traditional English- and Irish-style beers that have been made for centuries. The operation's motto is the Gaelic phrase "*Ni neart go cur le cheile*," which translates to "No strength without unity." The brewery's top-selling Irish red is called O'Ruaidhri's (pronounced "O'Rory's"). Its other beers have been named to match the brewery's Irish theme, like the Dullahan Celtic Headless Horseman coffee porter, Clíodhna the Goddess apple ale and the Daiker's Wee Heavy. The brewery's flagship malt-forward pale ale is named after Hayes's grandmother Stella.

Hayes Public House expanded its facility and production capabilities in 2015, 2016 and 2017. Its business plan has been ahead of schedule with continued growth. Hayes's beers are now distributed on tap in Central Minnesota, as well as in Irish pubs throughout the state. Hayes has become a model and inspiration for other small, community breweries throughout Minnesota.

Urban Lodge Brewing

For two years, between 2016 and 2018, Sauk Rapids had its own brewpub. While the location known as Urban Moose, or Urban Lodge, has since closed and become a Mexican restaurant, the establishment is remembered fondly. Urban Lodge helped spread a new beer culture in Central Minnesota. Brewing at the facility may someday resume—the regional El Loro chain that now operates the space and owns all of the old Urban Lodge recipes has publicly said it wants to add a *cerveceria* (brewery) to the space.

Urban Lodge was the vision of storied restaurateur Roy Dodds. He grew up in Mound and attended culinary school at Hennepin Technical College. Dodds had a long career in fine dining and high-end catering before deciding to open his own Sauk Rapids pizzeria in 2012. Dodds wanted to cook for the common man and give a chef's perspective to one of America's most popular foods. He opened Flying Pig Pizza, which quickly earned rave reviews for its specialty pies. Flying Pig served up toppings like tater tots, mashed potatoes, macaroni and cheese, chicken and wild rice, enchiladas, a Reuben and Jamaican jerk chicken. As appetites for craft beer began to expand across Central Minnesota, Dodds got the idea to expand his successful pizzeria. The bulk of Flying Pig's business came from its delivery and carry-out service, and a brewpub would offer the restaurant the opportunity to expand its dine-in and bar business.

The idea of Urban Moose Brewing Co. was born while Dodds was initially scouting locations along the Mississippi River; the eventual location was an old American Legion building in Sauk Rapids that had closed about a year earlier. Dodds hired head brewer Kevin Clark to run the brewery's initial fifteen-barrel system. Clark was previously brewing at Monterey, California's Peter B's Brewpub. Dodds closed Flying Pig Pizza in April 2016 with the plan to move and incorporate it into the new brewery. Urban Moose was opened in July 2016, with Neapolitan pizzas, appetizers and a tap lineup of a blonde, IPA, imperial IPA, stout, saison, wheat, hefeweizen and Belgian gold. Urban Moose was the first commercial Sauk Rapids brewery to open since the Sauk Rapids Brewing Co. and Eagle Brewing brewery burned down on February 14, 1895.

A few months after Urban Moose opened its doors, the brewery changed its name. Urban Moose received a trademark complaint from Canada's Moosehead Brewery—an establishment that was founded in 1867 and run by six generations of the Oland family. Moosehead is considered Canada's oldest independent brewery and has long been known for its Moosehead lager. Actor Michael J. Fox famously gave Moosehead a shout-out on the *Jay Leno Show*—newspaper reports say that he later received a truckload of Moosehead beer for the national television plug. Moosehead complained that having another brewery with "Moose" in its name could be misleading to customers. In December 2016, Urban Moose announced that it would be renamed Urban Lodge Brewing. Dodds told the *St. Cloud Times* that the trademark dispute was a blessing in disguise and gave the brewery an opportunity to brand itself as a brewpub.

After eighteen months of business, Dodds put Urban Lodge up for sale when he was diagnosed with a rare lung disease. Dodds also cited the crowded restaurant and bar market as a part of his decision to put the business up for sale in a WJON online report. Dodds kept Urban Lodge operating and brewing beer while he sought a buyer. News broke in late August 2018 that Dodds had sold Urban Lodge. A week later, Urban Lodge opened and closed its doors for a final time with its send-off celebration. El Loro Restaurant Group purchased the space, and the regional Mexican restaurant chain—which has long operated a number of locations in the Twin Cities and opened its first Central Minnesota location in Waite Park a year earlier—moved in. El Loro soon announced its intention of brewing at the site. The restaurant was remodeled for nearly a year before it was opened in Sauk Rapids in July 2019. The brewery portion is still a part of the restaurant's plans, but it remains unopened as of this book's publication.

Starry Eyed Brewing

The last remnant of Little Falls's storied brewing history was lost in 1983, when the old brewery that housed the Kiewel and Grain Belt operations was demolished by the city. But the old brewing culture of Little Falls was revived in 2017, when Starry Eyed Brewing opened in the city along the Mississippi River.

The brewery was founded by high school friends Thomas Goebel Jr. and Kyle Kieffer. According to a *Growler Magazine* report, the two talked about starting their own Little Falls brewery for several years. Goebel had previously worked at Minneapolis's popular Indeed Brewing and had studied brewing at the prestigious Siebel Institute. Goebel focused on recipe creation and beer production. Kieffer had been running his own excavating company since 2000 and handled the business and sales side of the brewery.

The Starry Eyed's unique name and artistic logo, which is on display in its taproom, has a deep and emotional meaning. The brewery was named and designed in honor of Goebel's late wife, Dayna, who passed in 2014 after a four-year battle with pancreatic cancer. Dayna had gifted Goebel with his first homebrew kit a decade before Starry Eyed Brewing was opened. While battling cancer, Dayna had encouraged Goebel to pursue his dream of having a professional brewing career. The Starry Eyed logo was inspired by a photo of Dayna. "She loved stars," Goebel said in a *Growler Magazine* interview. "She was a big fan of stars and she was a very, very optimistic person, right through cancer and everything."

Goebel and Kieffer converted an old six-thousand-square-foot welding and repair shop into the Starry Eyed brewery and taproom. The space opened in September 2017, with a cream ale, white, blonde, wheat, amber, IPA, double IPA, robust porter, saison and ESB. The Morrison County Historical Society's research said it was the county's first brewery in more than five decades. Starry Eyed is sharing its beer well beyond Morrison County; the brewery distributes to taps throughout the state, including those in Central Minnesota and the Twin Cities.

Rustech Brewing

Monticello's first-ever brewery was born out of an eclectic vision of honoring both technology and history. Both inspirations are very present in the 105

West Third Street brewery and taproom, which was opened in May 2018. Rustech Brewing—a clever title pronounced like "rustic"—is decorated with steampunk décor, including pipes, pulleys, old dials and historic farm wood. The brewery also has plenty of technology, including custom-designed brewing software and TV screens that show pictures of the brewing process and showcase the establishment's Untappd ratings.

Technology is what first turned Rustech Brewing's co-founders and Illinois natives, Bill and Penny Burt, on to brewing in the first place. Bill had long worked in software development when he was asked by a homebrewing coworker to build a system that would regulate temperatures during the brewing process. To test out the software, Bill taught himself how to homebrew and built his own system in his Monticello garage. "When he puts his mind to something, he works hard to make it perfect," said Penny of her husband. While it wasn't his initial intention to become a brewer, Bill fell in love with the homebrewing process, and an obsession formed. He later taught Penny—a longtime stay-at-home mom—how to homebrew. They both fell in love with recipe development, and many of their homebrews became inspirations for eventual Rustech Brewing beers.

The Burts became well-known homebrewers in their subdivision neighborhood, and during their neighborhood's regular block parties, they supplied beer for the festivities. "Our neighbors were our first taste testers," Penny said. "The neighborhood continues to support us so much to this day." While the Burts' homebrew obsession grew, Bill's brewing software system went commercial. Big Lake's Lupulin Brewing used his software during one of its expansions. This progress, combined with the Burts' only child, James, graduating from high school and heading off to the military, left empty-nesters Bill and Penny wondering if they should open their own craft brewery in Monticello. They began consulting Lupulin and Elk River's AEGIR Brewing for advice.

Before Rustech Brewing was born, the Burts had to change Monticello laws that prohibited breweries. Monticello was founded in 1856 but had never previously housed a commercial brewery, even in the days before Prohibition. The city's name was derived from the Italian word for "little mountain" and "small hill." Monticello is located along the Mississippi River in northern Wright County and is situated between St. Cloud and the Twin Cities. The Burts found the City of Monticello easy to work with and eager to add its own community brewery.

Rustech Brewing was opened to much fanfare on Memorial Day weekend 2018. The taproom, which is visible off of the heavily trafficked

Highway 25, brought the craft beer culture to the growing city. Rustech Brewing debuted with an IPA, wheat and blonde on tap. The brewery later released a blueberry cream ale called Blue Polar, which has since become incredibly popular—during its debut the brewery sold out of all 233 pints in less than two days. Fruit flavoring is also a part of Rustech Brewing's best-selling beer—a raspberry habanero wheat beer based on one of Penny's homebrew recipes.

Bill has maintained his software job but handles a majority of Rustech's brewing. He's also been mentoring assistant brewer John Thrailkill. Penny has been managing the taproom and the front of the house; she books food trucks, musicians and other events at Rustech Brewing. "The community has been so excited and supportive," Penny said. "Not just for the beer but to have something like this in town that brings in different aspects of food and entertainment."

NORDIC BREWING

Monticello got a second brewery when Nordic Brewing opened in November 2018. The founders of the operation not only bonded over beer but also shared a love for fantasy fiction, like *The Lord of the Rings* and *The Chronicles of Narnia*. Head brewer Matt Belz teamed with Laura Belz and Zach Barthel in formulating the plan for the brewery.

Nordic Brewing beers all have a fictional backstory attached to them. The brewery's main logo is a wild, mountain goat–like animal called an ibex. The beers all have descriptions pertaining to the journey of the ibex. The story of the brewery is on its website and marketing materials: "Atop the highest mountain, by the light of the moon, the all-knowing Ibex awakes, thirsty from his dream. He calls out for three heroes to embark on one impossible quest…to craft him the perfect beer.…Will they succeed? Join them on their journeys, mishaps and conquests."

Nordic Brewing also pays homage to Minnesota's Scandanavian roots, with ski poles and rackets decorating its walls. Nordic Brewing opened with a pineapple ale, chocolate brown ale and cream ale. Nordic Brewing has gone on to experiment with various styles and gives Monticello residents and travelers a second brewery to enjoy.

13
RESTAURANTS THAT SPECIALIZE IN BEER

Just as breweries have popped up in Central Minnesota, more and more restaurants' tap lines in the area have been dedicated to craft beers. Some places go above and beyond to fill their taps with craft beer. After being responsible for covering the Central Minnesota restaurant scene for multiple years, this book's author has gotten to know the true craft beer gems of Central Minnesota. If you are looking for a tasty meal paired with a wide selection of quality craft beers, consider these Central Minnesota spots.

St. Cloud

White Horse at 809 West St. Germain Street

Late White Horse founder Brian Lee was always a light beer drinker, until one day when he tried a then-relatively small and unknown Surly Brewing beer in July 2008. Years later, he referred to that moment as an "epiphany" in discovering craft beer. The evening after tasting Surly for the first time, Lee emailed Surly founder Omar Ansari. The next day, the two talked on the phone. While, at the time, Surly was operating solely in Brooklyn Center and was not distributing to Central Minnesota, the White Horse could serve Surly beer if its employees drove to pick it up themselves. Lee was so determined to get Surly on tap that he bought a pickup truck and started picking up kegs of Surly beer within a week of first trying it. Surly has since gone on to be on tap throughout Central Minnesota, but the White Horse was the first to bring the beer to the area. The White Horse was also one of the earliest establishments to add craft beers, and it continues to tap an excellent selection. Lee, unfortunately, tragically passed after a short battle with cancer in August 2017 at the age of sixty-three.

Lee's legacy continues on at the beloved White Horse in downtown St. Cloud. Opened by Lee in 2008, the White Horse serves up a diverse menu, with numerous cultural influences. Its menu offers standard bar food, like burgers, pizza and wings, but it also offers entrées with Thai, Indian, German, Greek, Korean, Italian and other inspirations.

Boulder Taphouse at 3950 Second Street South

When two production breweries returned to St. Cloud in 2014 and 2015, one St. Cloud beer bar hosted both of their debuts. Boulder Taphouse helped launch both Lupine Brewing and Beaver Island Brewing. Boulder Taphouse was opened in 2011 in an old Timberlodge Steakhouse. The Taphouse's business model included providing several dozen rotating beer taps, and it bet that a thirst for craft beer was on the horizon. Other Boulder Taphouse locations have been launched elsewhere in Minnesota and Iowa.

Boulder Taphouse was the vision of the successful Letnes Restaurant Group. Brothers Steve and Curt Letnes first tasted success with their St. Cloud creation Bonanza and later with a wood-fired grill concept called Grizzly's. The owners expanded that restaurant chain throughout Minnesota and the upper Midwest. Their managing partner, Ray Herrington, also helped build the Boulder Taphouse concept. In addition to its more than forty choices of beer, Boulder Taphouse serves up numerous fried appetizers, like cheese curds; more than a dozen wing sauces and dry rubs; specialty and build-your-own burgers; tacos; salads; and sandwiches.

7 West Taphouse at 28 Fifth Avenue South

Another Letnes Restaurant Group creation sits in downtown St. Cloud. Opened in December 2015, 7 West Taphouse operates out of an old record shop called the Electric Fetus. The bar has fifty taps reserved for a rotating selection of craft beers and serves up more than a dozen specialty burgers. The menu also includes salads, tacos and appetizers. The restaurant's French fries are freshly cut before being deep fried, and the food is quite economically priced. Other 7 West Taphouse restaurants are located throughout Minnesota—including a pair in Duluth—and a location in Wisconsin.

House of Pizza at 19 Fifth Avenue South

Few things pair better than beer and pizza. One of Central Minnesota's oldest pizzerias was also one of the earliest restaurants in the area to get craft beer in its taps. The House of Pizza was founded by Bob Testa in 1965, and it was opened under the name of a now-defunct Chicago pizzeria run by his family. More than fifty years later, the same six-shelf rotating pizza oven—that moves like a Ferris wheel—is used to cook pies in St. Cloud, and the legend of the House of Pizza lives on.

Bob's son, Brandon, has since taken over the family business and added a second location in Sartell in 2004. A third location, at 4040 Second Street in St. Cloud, was in the works at the time this book was written. The House of Pizza offers multiple crust styles, but it is overwhelmingly known for its thin crust variety, which is cut into squares. The House of Pizza has also become known for its cream cheese pizza topping don't knock it until you try it. The restaurant has trademarked its homemade recipes for its red sauce and sausage topping. The pizzeria keeps a wide selection of craft beers on tap and hosts numerous beer events and tap takeovers.

MC's Dugout Bar and Grill

St. Cloud State alumni may be familiar with this storied old college hangout. MC's is known for its novelty alcoholic concoction called the Hairy Buffalo, which is a mix of four liquors, orange juice and grenadine. Other Buffalo varieties—dirty, white tropical, Irish and Husky—are also available. Outside of the high-alcohol Buffalo drinks, MC's also dedicates a ton of its tap space to craft beers. Many of the craft beers are available in pitchers—meaning that it is a great stop for small groups. The MC's menu includes traditional bar food—appetizers, burgers and sandwiches—and the restaurant hosts regular four-course food and beer pairings and weekly bar events, like trivia.

SAUK RAPIDS

Old Capital Tavern at 2 North Benton Drive

This chef-driven restaurant was opened in June 2012 and provides Central Minnesota with a truly unique dining experience. Creator Aaron Salzer had previously operated Tavern on Germain in downtown St. Cloud. Salzer took a much different approach with Old Capital, named in honor of the local legend that says Sauk Rapids was in the running to be Minnesota's state capital until an 1884 tornado destroyed the town. Unique craft beers are put on tap, along with a wide whiskey selection; thought and care went into developing the beer tap lists. The restaurant operates in a 1915 building that was originally a bar but later became a car dealership and flower shop after Prohibition.

While the restaurant's first online review complained of its omission of Miller Lite and cheeseburgers from its menu, Old Capital has become a favorite of Central Minnesota foodies. The Old Capital menu has diverse options and rotates seasonally to keep the freshest ingredients in stock. Smoked meats are a trademark of the operation, and the kitchen has experimented with unique ingredients, including peacock meat. The restaurant even ages and cellars beers itself. Old Capital celebrated its fifth anniversary in 2017, with a block party featuring the '80s rock band Quiet Riot and a country group called Little Texas as headliners. Old Capital also does a lot of catering in the area.

Jimmy's Pourhouse at 22 Second Avenue North

Jimmy's Pourhouse is one of the most storied establishments in Sauk Rapids. The bar, which was opened in 1977 by Jimmy Lynch, replaced the old Blue Eagle Bar. Jimmy's has long been known by Central Minnesotans for its green-colored beer. Jimmy was born in Canada to Irish immigrants, so he tapped into his heritage and hosted an annual St. Patrick's Day festival. The tradition includes corned beef and an Irish stew recipe that's been passed down in Jimmy's family for generations.

Jimmy passed away in 2013, but his family has carried on his legacy—St. Patrick's Day is still the restaurant's busiest day of the year. Jimmy's has also added more taps and a quality beer selection; some local breweries have debuted their beers at the bar. The restaurant's menu includes a variety of appetizers, salads, burgers, entrées, sandwiches and baskets. The restaurant has long had its own trademarked hamburger bun recipe and has used the slogan "Nicest Buns in Town." Jimmy's also serves breakfast.

Sartell

G-Allen's at 116 Evergreen Drive

Since its opening in 2004, this sports bar and restaurant has long been ahead of its time when it comes to beer. G-Allen's was built on the idea of having a wide beer selection. Giant TVs and pool tables keep guests entertained. and a large tap line features a beer style for just about everyone. G-Allen's also has a diverse menu, with half-pound burgers, wings, sandwiches, wraps, pizzas, pastas and entrées. A late-night food menu is also available at the restaurant until 2:00 a.m.

ABOUT THE AUTHOR

Jacob Laxen is a former award-winning *USA Today* reporter who worked for the *St. Cloud Times* newspaper during separate stints, from 2007 to 2010 and from 2014 to 2016. The St. Cloud State University graduate traveled to the many communities of Central Minnesota in search of good beer and stories. He also covered craft and domestic beer nationally. Laxen now covers the beer scene in Fort Collins, Colorado, but teamed with local homebrew pioneer Bruce LeBlanc and photographer Andrew Webster to make this book.